DESTITUTE GOURMET

DESTITUTE GOURMET

SOPHIE GRAY

PHOTOGRAPHY BY TODD EYRE

Over 80 affordable and tasty new recipes plus fan favourites

CONTENTS

INTRODUCTION

If the phrase 'budget cooking' sends a shudder down your spine, then you are in good company. Frankly I'd rather stick a fork in my own eye than prepare meals that make me feel depressed before I've even eaten them. I want to cook and eat tasty, healthy, fashionable food that doesn't cost a fortune. Not 'budget' but 'within our budget'.

My *destitute gourmet* approach to cooking is influenced by a firmly held belief that good food is much more than just fuel with flavour. The place it holds in our lives is complex, like a language, and consciously or unconsciously we use it daily to express love or respect, convey status, celebrate, grieve, comfort, even punish. Food can be an addiction or an act of worship, and at the same time it remains one of life's simplest pleasures. The hot chips scoffed with the kids in a carpark after a blustery winter walk on the beach or the tray of home baking left on the doorstep on the day of your mother's funeral nourish in ways that no amount of fine-dining ever can. So it's no surprise, really, that shopping for food is as much an emotional issue as it is a financial or nutritional one, fraught with traps and habits that can become very expensive.

Unconscious and emotional overspending on food robs us of the opportunity to indulge in some of the other important and meaningful things in life, and piles on additional stress when money is tight. I know this from personal experience, having navigated through more than my fair share of tough financial times – including, most recently, the loss of my job to Covid-19 in the first frightening days of lockdown. But I also know that by using the following three *destitute gourmet* principles to strategically attack the grocery spend, we can still eat cracking good meals while saving a significant amount of money. That money can then be applied to some of those other important areas in life, which is empowering rather than depressing.

Below is a brief summary of the *destitute gourmet* principles and how they work, with some useful tips to kick you off. But if you are really serious about reducing your grocery bills, head to my website, www.destitutegourmet.com, where you'll find loads more practical information about how to maximise your savings.

1 **Shop smart.** Make a menu plan for the week and stick to it, set a budget for groceries that leaves you with some surplus, shop with a list, don't be afraid to try cheaper brands, avoid buying ready-made versions of things you can easily make yourself. Avoid waste with good planning and storage, and only shop once a week.

2 **Eat healthily and in season.** Peak-of-season produce is cheap, and health care is expensive, so bulk out your meals with veggies; learn what's in season and choose recipes that are seasonally appropriate, rather than because they're part of your routine or because the kids like them. Veggie up your meals, include fruit with snacks, learn how to store the surplus.

3 **Make a little bit of something luxurious go a long way.** If using a luxury ingredient, make sure it's working hard. Differentiate between essentials and luxuries; this varies from one household to another, but some things are common for all. For example, milk is pretty much essential for everyone, while fizzy drinks

are a luxury. Nobody actually needs fizzy drinks. In my house real coffee is an essential – I need it to survive – but we often skip meat because that works in our family. Being selective about treats and ruthless about other non-essentials releases funds for a good range of essentials to make a wide variety of meals. And it also makes it possible to save a significant sum each week, which can be redirected into those other important areas such as debt reduction, education, leisure or even a luxury ingredient for next week's menu.

GETTING STARTED

What are you currently spending each week? Add up the till receipts and then check your bank statements for additional purchases such as takeaways, drinks from the service station, café visits, etc. Tally it all up, and, when you have regained consciousness, work out how much you can actually honestly afford to spend on feeding your household. Then, using the *destitute gourmet* principles, cherry-pick the suggestions and techniques that will work for your family and lifestyle so that you can continue to eat well and also stay within your budget. Set some goals, get the family on board and get started.

In my opinion, the single most useful thing any household wanting to reduce their grocery spend can do is the first part of principle number 1: MAKE A MENU PLAN FOR THE WEEK AND STICK TO IT. If you do nothing else but that, you'll save some money. No extra takeaways or top-up shops will be needed, and after a few weeks you'll work out which are your most economical and successful dishes, which days are your toughest timewise and what just doesn't work for your household.

Do make a shopping list – a proper one that factors in breakfasts, lunches and all the ingredients needed to make the dishes on the menu – then check to see whether key items are in season or on special and then look in the freezer and pantry to make sure you aren't doubling up. Keep your list in or near the pantry so that when you finish the last of something you can immediately write it on the list, avoiding the always-expensive, last-minute, emergency top-up shop.

Prioritise your grocery money in this order, and gradually build up your stock of ingredients:

1 Vegetables and fruit. You can make a wider variety of nourishing food by combining fresh fruit and veggies with the odds and ends in your pantry than by spending money on anything else. Even if it means a week of porridge with fruit, and simple veggie soups, scones, pizzas and fritters to tide you over till pay day, a supply of produce will take you further than anything else. Choose some vegetables that can be eaten both raw and cooked for variety, like cabbage, carrots, celery or capsicum, along with the basics like onions, potatoes, kumara, pumpkin, spinach, cauliflower, apples, mandarins or kiwifruit . . . Include frozen options, too: stir-fry veg, mixed veg, peas, etc.

2 Staples such as flour, rice, oats, eggs, milk, butter/spread, cheese, oil, baking powder and baking soda, sugar, dried pasta . . . These basic staples combined with fresh produce can create an infinite number of tasty dishes and desserts.

3 Canned foods, seasonings and sauces take the basics from edible to palatable and on to delicious. You might add a sauce or a seasoning each week if you can afford it, gradually building up a stock of what you actually know you'll use.
4 Meat is a matter of personal choice and may need some negotiation in your household. Choose cuts you can afford and use recipes that make them go a long way. Minced meats, corned beef, chicken and pork are all at the more affordable end. Choose good, flavoursome sausages and use them as an ingredient rather than a meal; I freeze them in packs of three for using in risottos, sauces and pasta dishes. Use bacon as an ingredient rather than a meal, too; freeze in packages of 3–4 rashers so that it's on hand when needed. Fish is a luxury ingredient for us, but may be a cheap meal if fishing is your hobby.
5 Cleaning products can cost you dearly. You need to clean the bath, the loo, the bench and the floors, but dangly things for the loo and scented sprays for every room are not essential. Washing machine and dishwasher tablets are expensive if you are only doing a small load, whereas powders or liquids allow you to use only as much as you actually need (which may be less than they suggest on the pack). And what about the pets – are you buying premium pet food but skimping on yourself?

EXTRA TIPS AND TRICKS

1 Snack-size resealable bags are ideal for freezing small amounts of cream, wine, etc. so that you have these on hand when you need to slosh some into a sauce. I wash the bags well and reuse them multiple times.
2 Bread is among the most frequently wasted foods, so keep a bread bag in the freezer for those bits that are usually headed for the bin. In recipes that call for breadcrumbs, you can definitely swap slices for crusts – no one will know the difference.
3 Buy up on specials, but don't go crazy. There is little value in having a freezer overstuffed with chunks of things you never fancy eating but not enough money for a doctor's appointment. Buy only things that you *know* you'll use. Specials come around in cycles, so try to buy your luxury ingredients when they're on special.
4 Keep a roll of cling film in stock so that when you open a jar or can, you can dollop the remainder onto the cling film, wrap it up and freeze it immediately.
5 Stickers are handy for labelling things for the freezer. Another advantage of resealable plastic bags is that you can freeze things flat and stack them. They also take up less space and defrost much more quickly than containers, and you can actually see what's in them.

ABOUT THE INGREDIENTS

Seasonings are normally the least expensive part of a dish, so there is no excuse for bland food. I try not to use really obscure ingredients, but there may be some sauces or condiments that you don't currently keep in stock that I believe are worth investing in.

1 Dark soy sauce is a good source of umami – the fifth taste after sweet, salty, bitter and sour. It's that savoury, satisfying depth of flavour that makes you want to come back for more. I use an inexpensive common brand of dark soy sauce.

2 Kecap manis is a thick glossy sauce likened to sweet soy sauce. Although you can sometimes substitute with soy sauce and brown sugar, it's not the same. I use it in stir-fries and Asian dishes.

3 Shaoxing wine tastes much like sherry but has less alcohol, so little that in the supermarket you'll find it with the Asian ingredients, not the wine. It's cheap and gives an authentic flavour to dishes.

4 Oyster sauce and hoisin sauce are useful for adding intensity and depth and can often be used interchangeably.

5 Fish sauce is one of those miraculous ingredients that really elevates the flavour of a dish. Used carefully it won't actually make the dish taste fishy, just 'better'.

6 Tomato sauce has quite a complex flavour profile. If you've ever made your own, you'll likely have included lots of spices, sugar, seasonings, etc. So on that basis it makes sense that a slosh of tomato sauce is an easy way to add a load of flavour in one hit. When using it as an ingredient, I buy the cheapest one I can find.

Fresh herbs are not just a garnish – they add tons of flavour and a decent hit of antioxidants to a dish.

At the very least, grow some parsley and mint in a pot if you haven't any garden. Oregano and thyme are really hardy, so pretty much look after themselves, and chives are also very forgiving. Coriander and basil are very temperature-sensitive; basil likes it hot and coriander likes the cool.

I usually buy a pot of a living herb from the supermarket, use it in a recipe, then plant the plant in the garden. When we didn't have a garden, I planted them in a home-made grow bag (a bag of compost with holes in, parked in a sunny spot and watered daily). I keep tubes of herb paste in the fridge for when fresh are scarce.

Fresh coriander is a somewhat polarising flavour; some people find it 'soapy'. I use it both as a flavour and as a garnish. If it's just a garnish, it will be marked as optional. If it's a key ingredient and you don't like it, there is no 'substitute', so you might be better off making something else.

Lemongrass comes as stalks, which can be frozen; they need chopping finely, which I find very annoying to do. It's also now available as a paste, which is a lot less fiddly, so I always keep some in the fridge.

Makrut lime leaves (formerly known as kaffir lime leaves) are incredibly fragrant and are like nothing else. The leaves are available in supermarkets; you only need a couple at any time and they can be frozen.

Dried herbs and spices are pantry essentials. A basic range should include basil, oregano, rosemary, sage, thyme and mixed herbs; cardamom, chilli (flakes and ground), cinnamon, coriander (seeds and ground), cumin (seeds and ground), curry powder, cloves, mixed spice, nutmeg, paprika, smoked paprika, ginger and turmeric.

Curry paste and a can of coconut milk are absolute essentials for me. I can create a meal that will suit virtually any diet from those key ingredients. Red curry paste is my go-to, but red or green are pretty much interchangeable. If you have loads of chillies, make your own and freeze it – I keep a jar in the fridge.

Stock is a vital part of many dishes. There is a lot of snobbery around stock, but frankly I am quite happy using stock powder for most things. There are a few dishes where a liquid stock will elevate the flavour, but in most cases if you have beef stock, chicken stock and veggie stock as powders you'll be fine. Buy gluten-free stock if you need it. As a general rule, I use one teaspoon of stock powder dissolved in one cup of boiling water, unless otherwise stated on the packaging.

Dried mushrooms provide a layer of savoury umami flavour, which is useful when there is no meat. A pack of dried mushrooms is cheap and will keep for ages.

Cheeses, and Parmesan in particular, contain lots of the amino acids like glutamate that provide the savoury flavours we crave. So the addition of Parmesan, like fish sauce, makes things taste better. Buy it on special and freeze it. Most cheeses can be frozen. I sometimes use a bit of mozzarella, more for fun than for flavour, as it's very mild-tasting. In most cases you can substitute mozzarella with your regular cheddar or Edam, unless it's the stretch you're after.

Milk has become much more complicated in recent years. You can often just swap in a non-dairy milk in baking with little noticeable effect. I use milk powder for some things, like home-made ricotta, as it's cheaper and is adequate for my purposes. If you want to give milk powder a whirl, make it up at night in a regular milk bottle and slip it into the fridge – the family will never notice the difference in the morning; just don't tell them.

Fresh fruit and vegetables are reasonably cheap unless you buy them out of season. Every year there is a beat-up in the media about the price of a tomato or a capsicum in August, when they are totally out of season. Eating seasonally is cheaper, supports our local growers and ensures that you have variety all year round. If you want a salad in winter, have a slaw, because lettuce and tomatoes are out of season but cabbage and carrots are cheap. Save the salsa for summer or make a fruit salsa from tangy tamarillos or pineapple instead.

Frozen and canned vegetables and fruit are a terrific way to ensure that you get plenty of variety regardless of the weather or season. The produce is packed so quickly that optimum nutrition is preserved, too, so using a bag of frozen stir-fry mix instead of an expensive broccoli is not compromising your nutrition in any way. I also use frozen berries for desserts and baking, as fresh are quite expensive where I live, even when in season.

THE MAIN EVENT

Most households have a handful of recipes that stick with them through the decades and a bunch of others that change regularly with fashion and food trends. It's no different in my house, except that I have many, many more – literally hundreds of recipes to try to choose from. So, when it came to narrowing down some of my favourites to include in this book, I simply could not make up my mind. In desperation I decided to ask the *destitute gourmet* online community which recipes from earlier books they'd most want to see in a cookbook their kids might leave home with (if they ever leave home). There were still too many to include, but with their help I whittled it down and selected only the ones that stood out by miles, along with some of my new current favourites which I really hope you'll enjoy.

CREAMY LEMON PEPPER CHICKEN

READY IN: 1 HOUR   SERVES: 4

- 1 tbsp store-bought lemon pepper seasoning
- 1 tsp paprika
- 4 bone-in chicken thighs, or other bone-in cut of chicken
- 1 tbsp butter
- 2 cloves garlic, crushed
- ¼ cup chicken stock
- zest and juice of 1 lemon
- 2 cups loosely packed baby spinach leaves, plus a handful extra to decorate (optional)
- ¼ cup cream, sour cream or crème fraîche
- ¼ cup grated Parmesan
- 3–4 slices of lemon (optional)

This is a really tasty dish, and one I sometimes make for visitors. I buy extra chicken when on special and tuck it away in the freezer, which keeps the overall cost down. Spinach is pretty price-stable all year.

1 Preheat the oven to 180°C. Combine the lemon pepper seasoning and paprika and sprinkle over the chicken pieces, coating them all over.

2 Melt the butter in a frying pan and brown the chicken on both sides. Remove and place in a heatproof baking dish.

3 Add the garlic to the pan and cook gently for 1 minute, then add the chicken stock, bring to a simmer and cook for 2–3 minutes until reduced by half. Stir in the lemon zest, juice, spinach, cream and Parmesan, and pour over the chicken pieces. Add lemon slices if using.

4 Bake for 35 minutes, or until chicken is cooked. Scatter with extra spinach leaves if using. Serve with seasonal veg and roast or mashed potatoes.

TIP: You can use boneless chicken breast cut into serving-size portions, instead of thighs.

PEANUT CHICKEN AND RICE

READY IN: 45 MINUTES SERVES: 4-6

- 1 tbsp oil
- 2 boneless, skinless chicken breasts, thinly sliced
- 1 onion, chopped
- 3 cloves garlic, crushed
- 400g can chopped tomatoes
- ¼ cup crunchy peanut butter
- 1 tbsp curry powder
- large pinch of dried thyme
- 3 cups chicken stock
- 1½ cups basmati or jasmine rice
- ½ tsp salt

This is a good Sunday night supper-type dish – you probably have everything you need in the pantry and freezer already. It's tasty and satisfying in a risotto-ish kind of way but with a bit more zing.

1 Heat the oil in a large frying pan and cook the chicken until sealed on both sides, then remove to a plate. Add the onion and garlic to the pan and cook till soft.

2 Return the chicken to the pan and mix in the tomatoes, peanut butter, curry powder and thyme, mixing well to disperse the peanut butter through the mixture. Add the chicken stock and bring to a simmer. Stir in the rice and salt.

3 Return the mixture to a simmer, stir once to ensure that nothing is sticking to the bottom of the pan, then cover and reduce the heat to low. Cook for 20–25 minutes until all the liquid is absorbed and the rice is cooked. Serve with a salad or green vegetables.

TIP: This is a great first family dinner for the kids to learn to make.

TAGLIATELLE WITH CHICKEN AND LEMON DRESSING

READY IN: 20 MINUTES SERVES: 4

- dried tagliatelle, fettuccine or spaghetti for 4 people
- 45g butter (not oil)
- 2 cloves garlic, crushed
- 2 tbsp lemon juice, or more according to taste – a couple of good squeezes at least
- 350g cooked boneless chicken, shredded
- generous handful of chopped parsley
- zest of 1 lemon

This dish is brilliant for making a little bit of chicken go a long way. It's light and fresh in flavour and makes good use of the leftovers from a roast chook. Alternatively, throw it together with some cooked bacon, canned tuna or cooked sausage. Zest the lemon before squeezing the juice – you add the zest at the end.

1 Cook the pasta according to the packet directions. Reserve ⅓ cup of the starchy pasta water, then drain the pasta.

2 While the pasta is cooking, make the lemon dressing. Melt the butter in large saucepan, and when foaming add the garlic and then the lemon juice.

3 Add the drained pasta, shredded chicken and chopped parsley and toss through the dressing. Add a splash of starchy water, the lemon zest and some more lemon juice if desired. Serve immediately.

TIP: Serve sprinkled with some grated Parmesan if you like.

ZESTY CHICKEN, FETA AND VEGGIE SPANAKOPITA SPIRAL

READY IN: 1 HOUR SERVES: 4–6

1½ tbsp butter
200g silver beet, spinach, cabbage or a combination, very thinly sliced
3 cloves garlic, crushed
200g feta
½ cup grated Parmesan (around 50g)
1 chicken breast, cooked and shredded (optional)
zest of 1 lemon
1 tbsp lemon juice
small pinch of ground nutmeg
1 egg, lightly beaten
salt and pepper
8 sheets filo pastry
50ml olive oil

GLAZE – OPTIONAL

1 egg, lightly beaten
sesame or poppy seeds

This dish is another clever way to make a little bit of cooked chicken go a long way. While spanakopita is traditionally meat-free and made with spinach, I've made it using various different combinations of green veg. Simply omit the meat if you want to make it meat-free.

1 Preheat the oven to 200°C. Melt the butter in a large frying pan and heat until bubbling, then add the prepared greens and garlic and cook gently, stirring occasionally, till tender, around 5 minutes.

2 Remove from the heat and crumble in the feta. Stir in the Parmesan, shredded chicken (if using), lemon zest and juice and nutmeg, and when cool mix in the beaten egg. Season with salt and pepper.

3 Clear the bench so that you can lay out four sheets of filo end-over-end, overlapping each by about 5cm. Brush the filo sheets lightly with half of the oil, then place the remaining four sheets on top and brush these with oil too.

4 Spoon the filling loosely along the near long edge of the pastry, leaving a couple of centimetres uncovered at either end. Fold the ends in to enclose the filling and gently and loosely roll the pastry into a long sausage shape. I find it easier with two pairs of hands. Form the sausage into a loose spiral, around 20cm in diameter. Don't worry about small cracks or splits.

5 Slip the spiral onto a greased baking tray. Brush with beaten egg, if using, or a little oil, then scatter with seeds if desired and bake for 40–45 minutes, or until golden brown. Serve hot.

TIPS: It's easier to roll and shape if you keep the filling a little bit loose.

You can use the mixture for filo parcels if you prefer.

STUFFED CRUST PIZZA WITH SAUSAGE

READY IN: 1 HOUR SERVES: 4

- 1 quantity of All-purpose Pizza Dough (page 24)
- 1 quantity of Tangy Pizza Sauce (page 24)
- 200g block of mozzarella
- 3 good herby sausages
- 2 cloves garlic, crushed
- pinch of dried oregano
- 1 onion, chopped
- 6 slices salami, torn
- a handful of olives
- 1 tbsp oil
- basil leaves, to decorate (optional)

This is the pizza that will make you a legend with the teenagers. I bake it in a springform tin, which prevents the stuffed crust from unrolling as it cooks. The topping is just one suggestion – you can top yours with any pizza flavour you like. Check out some of our favourite pizza toppings on page 26–27.

1 Prepare the pizza dough.

2 While the dough is rising, grease a 26cm springform cake tin and prepare the tangy pizza sauce.

3 Cut half of the mozzarella into slices and then into thick matchsticks. Grate the other half.

4 Split the skins of the sausages with a serrated knife and tip the filling into a frying pan. Cook the sausage meat, crumbling it with a potato masher as it cooks. When lightly coloured, add the garlic and cook until tender, then stir in the oregano.

5 Preheat the oven to 220°C. Place the base of the cake tin on the bench. Dust the bench with flour and roll the dough out to a circle approx. 30cm across. Lift the dough onto the tin base so that it overhangs evenly all the way around. Arrange the mozzarella sticks end to end around the overhang, then roll the dough tightly over the mozzarella to form a crust that fits within the base. Clip the cake tin ring into place to hold the dough in shape.

6 Spread the base with the tangy pizza sauce, then scatter on the chopped onion, sausage mixture, grated mozzarella, salami and olives.

7 Brush the crust with the oil and leave for 10–15 minutes, or until doubled in size. Reduce the oven temperature to 210°C and bake for 20–25 minutes, or until cooked. Serve scattered with basil leaves if desired.

TIPS: Try other fillings, such as leftover bolognaise or chilli con carne.

Serve with a jacket potato, and salad or slaw, for a hearty family dinner.

ALL-PURPOSE PIZZA DOUGH

READY IN: 25 MINUTES
MAKES: ONE 34CM THICK-CRUST PIZZA BASE OR TWO 30CM THIN-CRUST BASES

2½ cups plain flour
1 tbsp sugar
1 tsp salt
1 sachet instant yeast
2 tbsp olive oil
1–1½ cups warm water

This dough recipe can be doubled to feed a big family or to stock the freezer. Once made, the dough can be stored in the fridge for 3 days or in the freezer for up to a month.

1 In a large bowl or a mixer fitted with a dough hook, combine the flour, sugar, salt, yeast and oil. Mix lightly.

2 Gradually add the water, stirring continuously until the flour is moist enough to form a dough. Knead the dough for 3–5 minutes, adding more flour if needed to prevent the dough sticking, until it is smooth and elastic.

3 Place the dough in a clean, greased microwave-safe bowl and cover with cling film. Microwave on **low** power for 1 minute, rest the dough for 10 minutes, then repeat. After the second rest, the dough should have doubled in size. Alternatively, set aside in a warm place until doubled in size, 30–40 minutes.

TIP: For freezing, once the dough has risen, roll half the mixture into pizza bases to freeze. Smaller, single-serving-sized bases are easier to store as they can be stacked when frozen and are less likely to break. Defrost, then top them and bake as usual.

TANGY PIZZA SAUCE
⅓ cup tomato paste
¼ cup chutney

TANGY PIZZA SAUCE

The combination of tomato and chutney is both sweet and tangy, resulting in the sort of flavour you expect from pizza-chain pizzas but made fresh each time with nothing dodgy in there.

1 Mix together and spread onto a prepared pizza base.

NO ONION OR TOMATO BUT STILL VERY TASTY CAPSICUM AND SAUSAGE PIZZA

READY IN: 45 MINUTES SERVES: 4

- 1 quantity All-purpose Pizza Dough (see opposite)
- 3 herby meaty sausages
- 2 tbsp olive oil
- 2 cloves garlic, minced
- 1 tsp dried basil
- 1 tsp dried oregano
- ¼ tsp chilli flakes
- salt and pepper
- handful of pitted olives, sliced
- 1½ cups grated cheese
- 3 capsicums, deseeded and thinly sliced

This pizza is a good option for people who can't or won't eat tomato or onion. It also makes a few sausages into a full meal. When capsicum is out of season, you can use frozen or a jar of chargrilled capsicum.

1 Prepare the pizza dough. While the dough is rising, prepare the topping.

2 Split the skins of the sausages with a serrated knife and tip the filling into a frying pan. Brown the sausage meat, crumbling it with a potato masher as it cooks. Once browned, set aside off the heat. Combine the oil, garlic, herbs and chilli flakes in a small bowl. Set aside.

3 Preheat the oven to 220°C. On a lightly floured bench, roll out the dough to a circle approximately 33cm in diameter and transfer to a greased baking sheet. Pour the olive oil mixture over and spread with the back of a spoon. Season with salt and pepper.

4 Scatter on the sliced olives and 1 cup of the cheese. Top with the crumbled sausage, sliced capsicums and remaining cheese.

5 Bake for 10–15 minutes, until the base is crisp and cooked.

TIP: Add other pizza toppings of your choice, such as sliced mushrooms or other meats.

3 REALLY POPULAR PIZZA TOPPINGS

READY IN: 45–60 MINUTES SERVES: 4

Home-made pizzas are inexpensive and are often both tastier and healthier than bought ones. From the fancy stuffed crust (see recipe on page 22) to a kid-friendly classic like Hawaiian, pizza is a great option for informal entertaining, family dinners or feeding a load of kids at a sleepover.

My All-purpose Pizza Dough and Tangy Pizza Sauce are on page 24.

HAWAIIAN

1 quantity of All-purpose Pizza Dough
1 quantity of Tangy Pizza Sauce
½ onion, chopped
1 cup grated cheese or pizza cheese
2–3 rashers bacon, chopped (around 1/2 cup)
¼ cup pineapple chunks, drained and chopped
½ red capsicum, chopped

1 Prepare the pizza base, spread with the pizza sauce, then scatter on the onion, grated cheese, bacon, pineapple and capsicum.

2 Cook in an oven preheated to 220°C for 15 minutes, or until done.

BBQ CHICKEN

1 skinless, boneless chicken breast, cut into thin slivers
½ cup store-bought BBQ sauce
1 quantity of All-purpose Pizza Dough
1 quantity of Tangy Pizza Sauce
½ onion, chopped
½–1 cup grated cheese
1 rasher of bacon, chopped (optional)
½ red capsicum, chopped

1 In a bowl, combine the sliced chicken and half the BBQ sauce, stirring to coat.

2 Prepare the pizza base and pizza sauce. Combine the remaining BBQ sauce with the pizza sauce and spread over the base.

3 Scatter on the onion, cheese, chicken, bacon (if using) and capsicum.

4 Cook in an oven preheated to 220°C for 15 minutes, or until cooked. Serve drizzled with extra BBQ sauce if desired.

CHICKEN TIKKA PIZZA WITH MINTY YOGHURT SAUCE

This is a slightly more grown-up flavour profile, like a restaurant pizza – that said, my kids loved it.

1 large skinless, boneless chicken breast, thinly sliced
a good squeeze of lemon juice
1 tbsp ground coriander
1 tbsp ground cumin
1 tsp paprika
½ tsp ground chilli
3 cloves garlic, crushed
100ml plain unsweetened yoghurt
1 quantity of All-purpose Pizza Dough
1 quantity of Tangy Pizza Sauce
1 cup grated cheese or pizza cheese
½ capsicum, chopped

MINTY YOGHURT SAUCE

100ml plain unsweetened yoghurt
2 cloves garlic, crushed
a handful of mint leaves, finely chopped
a squeeze of lemon juice

1 Place the chicken in a bowl with the lemon juice, spices, garlic and yoghurt. Marinate for 20 minutes.

2 Prepare the pizza base, spread with the pizza sauce, then scatter with the cheese, marinated chicken and chopped capsicum.

3 Cook in an oven preheated to 220°C for 15–20 minutes, or until done.

4 For the Minty Yoghurt Sauce, combine all the ingredients and drizzle on top of the pizza when baked.

COWBOY CASSEROLE

READY IN: 40 MINUTES SERVES: 4-6

500g beef mince
½ onion, chopped
2 x 400g cans baked beans
½ tbsp Worcestershire sauce
½–1 tsp ground cumin
¼–½ tsp ground chilli
pinch of dried oregano
1 heaped tbsp tomato paste
1 tsp beef stock powder (or a beef stock cube)
1 cup dried macaroni, cooked and drained
1 cup grated cheese
salt and pepper

A fan fave, my Cowboy Casserole will have both adults and kids cleaning their plates. It's a great recipe for beginners to learn to make, too, as it doesn't require much skill or equipment.

1 Preheat the oven to 180°C. Heat a medium-sized saucepan and brown the mince, stirring and crushing with a masher or fork until crumbly. Add the onion and cook, stirring, until softened.

2 Stir in the beans, Worcestershire sauce, spices, oregano and tomato paste, then sprinkle in the stock. Mix well, then add the cooked macaroni and season with salt and pepper.

3 Pour into an ovenproof casserole-type dish and cover with the grated cheese. Bake till the cheese is melted and turning brown. Serve with salad, slaw or cooked seasonal veggies.

TIPS: More ambitious eaters might like to mix it up a bit by swapping a can of baked beans for chilli beans.

To make it gluten-free, use GF pasta and stock and check the beans – some brands aren't GF.

DEVILLED MEATBALLS

READY IN: 40 MINUTES SERVES: 6

500g beef mince
1 slice of bread, made into breadcrumbs
2 tsp dried mixed herbs
1 tsp salt
2 tbsp oil
½ cup finely chopped onion
½ cup grated apple
½ cup fruit chutney
1½ cups hot water
2 tsp beef stock powder
1 tbsp brown sugar
1 tbsp soy sauce
1 tbsp cornflour
3 tbsp cold water

This fan fave is a recipe I grew up with, my own kids loved it even as littlies, and we still enjoy it now. The sauce packs a lot of flavour and is excellent with sausages or a meatloaf, too.

1 In a bowl or processor combine the mince, breadcrumbs, herbs and salt. Using wet hands, form the mixture into bite-sized balls. Heat the oil in a large, shallow frying pan and fry the balls till lightly browned. Remove from the pan.

2 Add the chopped onion to the pan and fry gently till soft. Add the grated apple, chutney, hot water, stock powder, brown sugar and soy sauce and bring to a simmer, stirring.

3 Return the meatballs to the sauce and simmer for 15 minutes. Combine the cornflour and cold water and add this to the sauce to thicken it. We always serve this with rice and seasonal veg, but there is no reason why you couldn't serve it with creamy mashed spuds or even spoon it onto Yorkshire puddings.

TIP: For devilled sausages, brown sausages in the pan instead of meatballs, then continue making the sauce in the same manner. Simmer the sausages in the sauce until cooked through; serve with mashed potatoes.

3 THINGS TO STUFF INTO BURGER BUNS

READY IN: 30 MINUTES SERVES: 4-6

A burger is an easy go-to weeknight meal, and pretty much any burger filling can be repurposed to make a filling for tacos or be served crustless with a salad.

For a next-level burger, try making your own buns from the recipe on page 35. I usually add a pile of crispy home-made potato wedges – cheaper than bought wedges and healthier than chips. Find my recipe on page 120.

CRISPY CRUMBED FISH

Use for burgers, sliders or fish tacos.

2 cups panko breadcrumbs
½ cup plain flour
2 eggs, lightly beaten
450g white fish, cut into bite-sized portions
⅓ cup oil, for frying
burger or slider buns
aïoli, to serve
slaw (see page 121), to serve

1 Place the breadcrumbs, flour and beaten egg in separate shallow bowls.

2 Dip each piece of fish first in the flour, coating lightly, then in the egg and finally in the breadcrumbs.

3 Heat the oil in a frying pan and cook the fish till golden and crisp on both sides.

4 Assemble the burgers: split the buns, toast lightly and spread with aïoli, then add slaw, some crispy fish and extra aïoli.

TIP: You could serve the crispy crumbed fish and slaw with a jacket potato instead of buns, or in flour tortillas (see page 117).

SPICY COURGETTE PATTIES

3 medium-sized courgettes, grated
2 tsp store-bought curry paste
1 tsp grated ginger
1 tsp wholegrain mustard
1 egg
100g fresh breadcrumbs (around 2½ slices)
a big handful of coriander, roughly chopped
salt and pepper
2-3 tbsp oil, for frying
toasted burger buns
4 tbsp aïoli
lettuce, tomatoes, beetroot or other fillings of your choice
4 tbsp mango chutney

1 Place the grated courgettes in a clean tea towel and squeeze out as much liquid as you can. Tip into a bowl or processor and add the curry paste, ginger, mustard, egg, breadcrumbs and coriander. Season with salt and pepper and mix to combine.

2 Form the mixture into four patties. Heat the oil in a frying pan and fry the patties slowly and gently on each side until golden and firm. (Cook them too quickly and the moisture won't evaporate, leaving you with a soggy burger).

3 Spread the base of each burger bun with aïoli, then add lettuce, tomato, beetroot and any other of your preferred burger fillings. Add patties and spread each with a tablespoon of mango chutney. Place bun tops in position and skewer to hold them together.

TIP: You can make small patties from the mixture and use like falafel, or enjoy as a snack with mango chutney for dipping.

CLASSIC BEEF BURGERS

500g beef mince
2 slices of bread, made into breadcrumbs (approx. 1 cup)
½ onion, finely chopped
½ tsp salt
1 tsp dried mixed herbs
¼ cup tomato sauce
1 tsp soy sauce
2 tsp Worcestershire sauce
1 tsp beef stock powder
1 egg
toasted burger buns
salad ingredients or slaw
sauces of your choice

1 In a bowl or processor, combine the mince, breadcrumbs, onion, salt and herbs. Add the tomato sauce, soy sauce, Worcestershire sauce and stock. Break in the egg and mix well or pulse to combine.

2 Divide the mixture into 5 or 6 balls, then flatten to form patties suitable for the size for your buns. Bear in mind that they will shrink a bit when cooking.

3 Grill, fry or barbecue for approximately 4 minutes each side. Serve in a bun with salad or slaw and your preferred sauces – BBQ, tomato, aïoli . . .

HOME-MADE HAMBURGER OR HOT DOG BUNS

READY IN: 1½ HOURS
MAKES: APPROX. 16 BURGER OR HOT DOG BUNS, OR MORE IF YOU MAKE MINI SLIDER BUNS

5 cups plain flour
¼ cup sugar
2 tsp salt
1½ sachets instant yeast
1½ cups milk
1 cup cream
1 egg, lightly beaten
1 tbsp sesame seeds

Burgers get a bit of a bad rap, but a home-made burger is definitely *not* junk food. Store-bought buns are inexpensive and acceptable, but you can elevate the humble burger to new heights with home-made buns. I don't make these for every day, but for kids' birthdays and barbecues they definitely step up the standard. For three of my fave burger patties, see the previous three pages.

1 In a large bowl, combine the flour, sugar, salt and yeast. Heat the milk and cream together till warm but not hot. Pour into the flour mixture and beat with beater or a mixer fitted with a dough attachment for around 5 minutes, scraping down the sides of the bowl until all the flour is incorporated. You should have a smooth, elastic, slightly batter-like dough.

2 Transfer the dough to a clean, greased microwave-safe bowl and cover with cling film. Microwave on low power for 1 minute, rest the dough for 10 minutes, then repeat. After the second rest, the dough should have doubled in size. Alternatively, set aside in a warm place until doubled in size, approx. 40 minutes.

3 Grease two large baking trays. For burger or slider buns, punch the dough down and roll it out on a floured bench to approx. 1½ cm thick for sliders or 2½ cm thick for regular burger buns. Cut the buns using a suitably sized cutter (I use one that is 8cm for regular buns), and place on the trays. Brush with beaten egg and sprinkle with sesame seeds.

4 For hot dog buns, divide dough into 16 pieces, then roll each piece into a 15cm log. Place on trays and leave to rise until doubled in size. Brush with beaten egg and sprinkle with sesame seeds if desired.

5 Preheat the oven to 190°C. When buns have risen, bake for 20–25 minutes, or until golden brown. Rotate the trays as necessary to ensure even baking. Cool on a rack.

TIP: FYI, they're buns, not rolls, because they are much sweeter than a standard roll.

CRISPY BACON-WRAPPED PORK MEATLOAF

READY IN: 1 HOUR SERVES: 4-6

1 tbsp oil
1 medium-sized onion, chopped
2 cloves garlic, crushed
4 slices bread
1 egg, beaten
¼ cup milk
1 tsp salt
¼ tsp ground black pepper
1 tsp mustard powder or wholegrain mustard
1-2 tsp dried sage
500g pork mince
4-6 rashers of streaky or middle bacon, rind removed

This dish makes an excellent special-occasion meal. Serve it hot in thick slices with roast vegetables, or cold with salads and chutney. It has a lovely savoury flavour that appeals to diners of all ages, which makes it a good choice for family get-togethers. In our whānau there is always fierce competition for the crispy 'end cuts'.

1 Preheat the oven to 200°C. Heat the oil in a small pan and gently cook the onion and garlic till soft. Remove from the heat and set aside. Grease a rimmed baking tray with non-stick spray or rub with a little oil.

2 Tear the bread, crusts and all, into pieces and place in a large mixing bowl. Add the egg, milk, seasonings, mustard, sage and cooled onion and garlic. Mix with a fork till soft and mushy, then add the pork mince and mix well.

3 Place a sheet of foil on the bench and arrange the bacon slices side by side, stretching them out so they are quite thin. Arrange the pork mixture in a log shape down the middle of the bacon, leaving enough bacon each side to wrap around the log. Lift the sides of the foil and wrap them around the log so that the bacon encloses the sides of the 'loaf' and just wraps over on itself.

4 Place on the tray, unfold enough of the foil to expose the surface of the loaf where the bacon joins, then flip the loaf over so that this side is facing down. Reshape it gently, then peel off the foil. You should have a neat bacon-wrapped loaf.

5 Bake for 40 minutes, or until juices run clear when you pierce the loaf with a fork. This is good served with the smashed potatoes on page 119.

TIPS: When the loaf is cold, slice it thinly for an excellent sandwich filler!

This is an easy recipe to double for a family celebration, making two loaves, or to make as individual mini loaves for a dinner party.

I wash the foil in soapy water so that I can reuse it.

SPICY SMOKY SLOW COOKER PULLED PORK

READY IN: 6½ HOURS SERVES: 6

- ¾ cup store-bought tomato sauce (use a cheapo brand)
- 3 tbsp tomato paste
- 1 onion, finely chopped
- 2–3 fat cloves garlic, chopped
- ⅓ cup chipotle peppers in adobo sauce, chopped (see tips)
- ½ tsp smoked paprika
- ½ tsp paprika
- 1 tsp mustard powder
- 1 tsp ground cumin
- ¾ cup cider vinegar
- salt and pepper
- 1.5–2kg bone-in pork shoulder (depending on the size of your slow cooker), excess fat and skin removed
- wraps, slider buns or tortillas, and slaw, to serve

Pulled meat is tender and great for stuffing into sliders or tortillas (see pages 35 and 117). It also goes well with salad or good slaw (see page 121) for a lower-carb option.

1 Combine the tomato sauce, tomato paste, onion, garlic, chipotle peppers and spices in the bowl of a slow cooker. Add the vinegar and season with salt and pepper.

2 Season the pork shoulder all over with salt and pepper, then place it in the slow cooker and coat it with the sauce.

3 Cover and cook on **high** for 5–6 hours or on **low** for 8–10 hours, until very tender. Turn the pork once or twice during the cooking time. When done, the meat should pull apart easily using a fork.

4 Remove the pork from the slow cooker and transfer to a bowl. Shred with two forks, removing the bones and any fatty lumps, then return to the slow cooker and mix into the sauce. Serve in wraps, buns or tortillas, with slaw.

TIPS: Chipotle peppers in adobo sauce are sold in small cans in the supermarket. They have a distinctive smoky flavour, and you can freeze the leftovers for next time.

If you want to remove residual fat from the dish, make it in advance and leave it to cool, then transfer it to a bowl and chill in the fridge for several hours. The fat will come to the surface and solidify, so can easily be lifted off. Reheat pork in the microwave, in a saucepan or in the oven (covered with foil), or return it to the slow cooker to reheat and serve.

FAMILY BARBECUE PORK SAUSAGE ROLL

READY IN: 55 MINUTES SERVES: 4-6

½ tbsp olive oil
1 onion, chopped
2 cloves garlic, crushed
3 rashers bacon, chopped
1 tsp dried sage
1 tsp mustard powder
½ tsp smoked paprika
450g pork mince
2 slices of bread, made into breadcrumbs
½ tsp salt
1 egg
½ cup store-bought BBQ sauce
2 sheets puff pastry, defrosted

GLAZE

1 egg, lightly beaten, or just use milk

My mother would have called this 'boy food' – savoury, filling and not too fancy. I like to use pastry trimmings to make the food look pretty, but you can skip that if it is too much faff and just enjoy a hearty, crispy, family-pleasing meal in under an hour.

1 Preheat the oven to 210°C. Heat the oil in a small pan and add the onion, garlic and bacon. Cook gently until soft, then stir in the sage, mustard and paprika and set aside off the heat.

2 In a bowl or processor, combine the cooked onion mixture, pork mince, breadcrumbs, salt and egg together. Add the BBQ sauce and stir till combined.

3 Join the pastry sheets together, sealing with a dab of water. Place on a greased baking tray and trim one-third off the short end of the pastry. Place the mince down the centre, brush the edges with water, roll, and fold in the ends to seal the roll.

4 Cut decorations from the remaining pastry and attach with a dab of water. Brush the roll all over with beaten egg or milk. Cut a few vents in the top to allow steam to be released, then bake for 30–35 minutes until dark golden. Serve as a family meal with roast spuds (see page 118) and green vegetables.

TIP: For a smaller household or a couple, divide the mixture and roll it into 6 sausage rolls, freezing any you don't use for a subsequent meal.

EASY HERBY FILO-TOPPED LAMB PIE

READY IN: 50 MINUTES SERVES: 4–6

500g lamb mince
1 onion, chopped
3 cloves garlic, crushed
1 carrot, finely chopped
200g mushrooms, chopped into chunks or quartered (1 cup of button mushrooms is around 100g)
2 stalks celery, finely chopped
1 tbsp chopped rosemary
1 tsp dried thyme
2 tbsp plain flour
1¾ cups beef stock
400g can 'Italian'-seasoned tomatoes
1 heaped tbsp tomato paste
salt and pepper
8 sheets filo pastry
¼ cup olive oil

This is a really versatile dish – it's easy to prepare, very savoury and can be made as individual pot pies or one family-sized dinner, whichever you prefer.

1 Preheat the oven to 210°C. Heat a frying pan and cook the mince, pressing with a potato masher or fork, until browned and evenly crumbly. Use a slotted spoon to remove the mince. Pour off all but half a tablespoon of the fat and return the pan to the heat.

2 Add the onion, garlic, carrot, mushrooms, celery, rosemary and thyme and cook gently, stirring occasionally, until the vegetables are becoming tender.

3 Return the lamb mince to the pan, then stir in the flour. Gradually add the stock, stirring continuously, then add the tomatoes and tomato paste. Season with salt and pepper and simmer until slightly thickened.

4 Pour into an ovenproof dish or individual ramekins. Brush each sheet of filo lightly with olive oil and crumple on top of the lamb mix. Bake for 35 minutes or until golden.

TIP: If you don't want to use filo, top the mixture with a creamy mashed potato or kumara topping, or cut tops for pot pies from a sheet of frozen puff pastry.

LAZY SUNDAY SAUSAGE RAGÙ

READY IN: 30 MINUTES SERVES: 4–6

500g dried pasta spirals, penne or shells
3-4 good herby sausages
1 red onion, chopped
3 fat cloves garlic, crushed
¼ tsp chilli flakes
1 tsp oil, if needed
2 tbsp tomato paste
400g can chopped tomatoes
½ tsp dried oregano
1½ tsp beef stock powder
salt and pepper
2 tbsp sour cream, crème fraîche or fresh cream
generous handful of chopped parsley

This is an easy, quick comfort-food dish; you need good sausages, but only a few of them. The blob of creaminess at the end enriches the dish, but you could leave it out or add some Parmesan instead. For extra decadence, serve with garlic bread (see page 124).

1 Bring a large pan of salted water to the boil and cook the pasta according to the packet directions. Reserve 1½ cups of the starchy water, then drain the pasta.

2 While the pasta is cooking, heat a frying pan, split the sausage skins with a serrated knife and squeeze the sausage filling into the pan. Cook gently, using a large fork or a potato masher to crumble the sausage meat as it cooks.

3 When the sausage meat is cooked, add the onion, garlic and chilli flakes and cook gently till the onion is soft. Add a drop of oil only if needed.

4 Stir in the tomato paste, canned tomatoes and oregano and cook for 2–3 minutes. Mix the stock powder into the reserved starchy water, add to the pan and simmer for a minute or two. Season with salt and pepper.

5 When ready to serve, add the sour cream and parsley and mix, then fold through the drained pasta and serve.

TIP: This is great with a chunk of garlic bread – turn to page 124 for the recipe.

HERBY PUMPKIN AND SAUSAGE GNOCCHI

READY IN: 45 MINUTES SERVES: 4–6

500g pumpkin, deseeded
2 tbsp olive oil
500g packet potato gnocchi
1 cup button mushrooms, cut into thick slices
3 good herby sausages
1 red onion, chopped
3 cloves garlic, crushed
½ cup chicken stock
1 cup cream or evaporated milk (see tips)
½ tsp dried sage
½ tsp dried Italian herbs
⅓ cup grated Parmesan
½ cup grated cheese

I can make my own gnocchi, but to be honest it's a bit of a palaver for a weeknight – so I use a pack of store-bought stuff from the supermarket in this dish. Use some mozzarella for the topping if you want a bit of stretchy action.

1 Preheat the oven to 210°C. Spray a rimmed baking tray with non-stick spray, or rub with a little vegetable oil. Peel the pumpkin and cut into 1½ cm pieces. Spread over the greased baking tray, toss with half a tablespoon of the oil and roast for 20 minutes, or until tender.

2 Cook the gnocchi according to the packet directions. Heat the remaining oil in a large ovenproof pan and cook the mushrooms until golden, then remove to a plate. Split the skins of the sausages with a serrated knife and tip the filling into the pan. Cook, mashing with a fork or masher until crumbled and turning golden, then mix in the onion and garlic and cook till soft.

3 Add the stock, cream, herbs and Parmesan, bring to a simmer and add the gnocchi. Simmer until beginning to thicken, then fold in the pumpkin and mushrooms. Transfer to an oven-safe dish and top with the grated cheese.

4 Bake in the preheated oven until golden on top. Serve with salad or cooked seasonal vegetables.

TIPS: This is one of those recipes that is easy enough for every day but also good enough for guests. You could easily divide the mixture into individual dishes for a more elegant presentation.

Evaporated milk provides a creamy alternative that you can keep in the pantry. Lite evaporated milk is lower in fat but won't thicken without a little added cornflour. If using evaporated milk, you need to take a little more care to ensure that it doesn't burn on the bottom.

CRISPY FISH PIE WITH CAPERS AND LEMON

READY IN: 1 HOUR   SERVES: 6

350–450g firm white fish (whatever is available)
approx. 300ml milk (enough to just cover the fish)
25g butter
50g plain flour
1 tbsp capers, finely chopped
3 gherkins, finely chopped
2 hard-boiled eggs, cooled and chopped
1 tbsp chopped parsley
squeeze of lemon juice
salt and pepper
2 sheets of frozen puff pastry, defrosted

This crispy pie is a fan favourite, and a number of people credit it with being responsible for getting their kids to eat fish. The addition of lemon, gherkin and capers gives a bit of zing, and a cup of cooked rice can be added to the filling to stretch it further if required.

1 Place the fish into a medium-sized saucepan and cover with the milk. Bring to a simmer and cook gently until the fish breaks apart when pulled gently with a fork, around 5–10 minutes. Place a sieve over a bowl and strain the fish, reserving 275ml of the milk.

2 In the same saucepan, melt the butter, then whisk in the flour and cook gently, stirring, for 1 minute. Now gradually incorporate the reserved milk the fish was cooked in, whisking well after each addition until you have a creamy sauce. Simmer the sauce for 5 minutes, then remove from the heat.

3 Break up the fish and add to the sauce with the capers, gherkins, eggs, parsley, lemon juice and salt and pepper to season. Mix gently, then set aside to cool completely.

4 Preheat the oven to 220°C. Grease a baking tray with non-stick cooking spray or rub with a little oil. Place one sheet of pastry on the tray and brush around the edges with water. Roll the second pastry sheet with a rolling pin to make it slightly larger than the first.

5 Spoon the cooled filling onto the pastry on the tray, then place the second pastry piece on top, pressing the edges firmly to seal. Slice 6 long vents into the pastry, brush it with a little extra milk and bake for 30 minutes, or until dark golden and puffed.

TIP: Make mini fish pies using the folding technique for Maharaja Pies on page 94, or put the filling in ramekins and top with filo or a creamy mash if you don't want to use pastry.

ONE-PAN WONDERS

If you are in a rush or simply don't have a lot of equipment or experience, a one-pan recipe is a great option. By definition, when I'm talking about a one-pan dinner, I mean a dish that doesn't require additional side dishes because it already includes both meat and vegetables, so can be served as is. I've also added a couple of one-pan breakfasts, since dishing up breakfast to everyone at the same time can seem nigh on impossible. The one-pan brekkies are tasty and fun to make – a good thing to roll out at the weekend or during school holidays so that the kids can learn how to make them.

Many recipes come down to a basic formula with interchangeable flavours and seasonings. Once you crack the code, you can use the same formula for a multitude of dishes. I use a large, cheap non-stick frying pan purchased from the supermarket and a baking tray in place of a lid for most of these.

Winner, winner, one-pan dinner!

CHEAP AND EASY CHICKEN MEE GORENG (SPICY FRIED NOODLES)

READY IN: 25 MINUTES SERVES: 4–6

MEE GORENG SAUCE

2 tbsp soy sauce
¼ cup kecap manis (see tips)
⅓ cup store-bought tomato sauce (everyday type)
3 tbsp sweet chilli sauce

FRIED NOODLES

300g dried noodles
1 tbsp oil
1 large skinless, boneless chicken breast, cut into thin strips
2 cloves garlic, crushed
1 tsp grated ginger
around 500g chopped veggies, or ¾ of a 750g bag of frozen stir-fry veggie mix
1–2 cups thinly sliced cabbage
3 eggs
juice of 1 lime or lemon
1 cup bean sprouts (optional)
fresh coriander, chilli and spring onion, to garnish (optional)

Fresh, filling and easy – skip the takeaways and make it better and cheaper at home. I use rice noodles, but you can use any kind; even 2-minute noodles are fine.

1 Make the sauce. Combine the ingredients in a small bowl and set aside. Prepare the noodles – soak and drain according to the packet directions.

2 Heat half the oil in a large frying pan or wok and stir-fry the chicken till cooked through, then remove from the pan.

3 Heat the remaining oil and add the garlic, ginger and vegetables (including cabbage). Stir-fry for 2–3 minutes till tender (if using fresh veg) or heated through (if frozen). Fold in the noodles and sauce and mix through until heated.

4 Return the chicken to the pan and continue to stir-fry. When piping hot, push the noodles and vegetables to the sides of the pan, making a well in the middle. Quickly break in the eggs and whisk with a fork, then remove from the heat and toss through the mixture. It should look glossy rather than scrambled-eggy.

5 Add a squeeze of lime or lemon juice and fold in the bean sprouts, if using. Add a handful of fresh coriander and spring onion, and a sprinkle of chilli if desired. Finish with another good squeeze of lime or lemon juice.

TIPS: Kecap manis is a type of sweet soy sauce; you can make a substitute version (see page 57).

You can use more chicken if you prefer, or swap the chicken for pork or beef mince.

SIAM CHICKEN AND RICE

READY IN: 45 MINUTES SERVES: 4-6

2–3 boneless chicken breasts, cut into thin strips
2 tsp sesame oil
2½ cups chicken stock
1½ cups basmati rice
¼ tsp salt
fresh chopped tomatoes, coriander and cashews, to garnish (optional)

MARINADE

3 Makrut lime leaves, halved
3 tbsp dark soy sauce
1 tbsp oyster sauce
3 cloves garlic, crushed
¼ tsp chilli flakes
2–3 tbsp chopped coriander
juice of 1–2 limes

You can also use this marinade for cooking chicken on the barbecue or slow-roasting in the oven.

1 Combine the marinade ingredients in a bowl. Add the sliced chicken and marinate for 10–20 minutes.

2 Heat a few drops of the oil in a large, heavy-based frying pan and cook the chicken a little at a time, adding another few drops of oil with each batch. Remove the chicken to a plate when sealed. When all the chicken is done, return it to the pan and add the stock, along with any marinade residue from the bowl.

3 Bring the mixture to a simmer, then stir in the rice and salt. Stir once to prevent the rice sticking, then cover with a baking sheet or lid, turn the temperature to its lowest setting and cook, without stirring, for 25 minutes.

4 Remove the lid, fluff with a fork and transfer to a serving platter. Discard the lime leaves and top with fresh chopped tomatoes, coriander and cashews, if using.

TIP: If tomatoes are out of season, omit them and add a couple of cups of frozen veg, or a scattering of green beans, before covering and cooking. I've also done the frozen veg version with pork mince in place of chicken.

GINGER SESAME CHICKEN AND GREENS

READY IN: 35 MINUTES SERVES: 4

½ tbsp sesame oil
450g boneless, skinless chicken thighs (or chicken breast), sliced
1 tbsp grated fresh ginger
4 whole cloves garlic, peeled
1 courgette, cut longwise then sliced
1¼ cups basmati rice
2½ cups liquid chicken stock (see tips)
3–4 cups seasonal greens – baby bok choy, beans, edamame, snow peas, kale or spinach . . .
½ cup chopped fresh coriander
1 tbsp sesame seeds, lightly toasted
sliced spring onion, to garnish (optional)

DRESSING

¼ cup sesame oil
¼ cup soy sauce

With a hint of Japanese influence, the flavour profile here is a bit more grown-up. I could eat it every day for the rest of my life – seriously, I love this dish.

1 Heat the oil in a large frying pan and cook the chicken in batches, removing to a plate when sealed. When all the chicken is done, return it to the pan and add the ginger, whole garlic cloves, courgette and rice and cook for 1 minute, stirring till the rice is mixed through.

2 Add the stock and bring to a simmer, stir once to ensure that nothing is sticking to the bottom of the pan, then cover with a lid, foil or a baking tray. Cook on low for 8 minutes.

3 Remove the cover, quickly scatter in the prepared greens, replace the cover and cook for a further 8 minutes. Check that the rice is cooked and the liquid has been absorbed. Rest off the heat, covered, for 5 minutes, then stir the coriander through.

4 Make the dressing by whisking the sesame oil and soy sauce together. Serve the rice, chicken and greens topped with a drizzle of the dressing, a good sprinkle of toasted sesame seeds and a scattering of spring onion if desired.

TIPS: Since stock is part of the clean flavour of this dish, it's one occasion when I might splash out on buying a liquid stock.

When adding the vegetables, re-cover the pan quickly to retain as much of the heat as possible. If using stalky vegetables such as broccoli or broccolini, cut the stems thinly for even cooking.

PEANUT PORK AND RICE

READY IN: 30 MINUTES
SERVES: 4 ON ITS OWN, OR 6 WITH A SALAD OR ADDITIONAL VEGETABLES

350–500g pork mince
1 finely chopped fresh red chilli, or ½ tsp chilli flakes
2 cloves garlic, crushed
1 tsp grated fresh ginger
1 carrot, peeled, halved longwise, then sliced into crescents
¼ cup (approx. 4 tbsp) crunchy peanut butter
3 tbsp kecap manis (see tip)
2 tbsp soy sauce
3 cups chicken stock
1¼ cups basmati or jasmine rice
3–4 cups chopped vegetables – fresh, frozen or a combo of both

GARNISH – OPTIONAL
chopped spring onion
handful of chopped peanuts
squeeze of lime juice

This family-friendly flavour combination is likely to become a staple.

1 Heat a large frying pan and brown the mince – I don't find it necessary to use any oil to do this. Press it with a fork or potato masher as it cooks, to crumble it.

2 When the mince is starting to brown, add the chilli, garlic, ginger and sliced carrot. Then stir in the peanut butter, kecap manis and soy sauce. You can add more chilli at the end when you taste the dish, just prior to serving.

3 Stir in the stock and rice, and mix to distribute the peanut butter throughout the mixture. Cover with a baking sheet or lid and simmer gently, without stirring, for 10 minutes.

4 Uncover, stir in the veggies, cover and cook for a further 15 minutes. Serve topped with chopped spring onion, peanuts and a squeeze of lime juice, if you have them.

TIP: If you don't have kecap manis, you can make a home-made version using equal parts of soy sauce and brown sugar, simmered together till syrupy with a little bit of ginger and a pinch of star anise.

LAMB BIRYANI WITH SPINACH

READY IN: 40 MINUTES SERVES: 4–6

450g lamb mince
1 tsp yellow mustard seeds
1 tsp cumin seeds
1 onion, chopped
2 tsp grated fresh ginger
2 cloves garlic, crushed
½ tsp chilli flakes
2 tbsp chopped curry leaves (see tips)
1 tsp each ground cumin, turmeric, garam masala
½ tsp ground cardamom
1 tsp salt
several chunks of frozen spinach
⅓ cup sultanas or raisins (optional)
1½ cups basmati rice
2½ cups beef stock
a dollop each of natural unsweetened yoghurt and chutney, to serve (optional)
handful of mint leaves, to garnish (optional)
1 tsp lightly toasted cumin seeds, to garnish (optional)

This curry is fragrant rather than spicy. You shouldn't need to add oil, as the lamb mince will release fat as it cooks, contributing to the lamby flavour in the dish.

1 In a large saucepan or frying pan, brown the mince, stirring and crumbling with a fork or masher as it cooks, until well browned.

2 With a slotted spoon, remove the browned meat to a bowl. Add the mustard and cumin seeds to the pan and heat, stirring, until they begin to pop.

3 When the seeds are popping, stir in the onion, ginger, garlic, chilli and chopped curry leaves, and cook gently, stirring occasionally, until softened. Add the remaining spices and cook gently for a minute or two.

4 Return the cooked meat to the pan and stir well, then toss in the frozen spinach and sultanas or raisins if using. Stir in the rice, mixing with the meat and spices, then add the stock and salt and bring to a simmer.

5 Once simmering, stir to ensure that nothing is sticking to the bottom of the pan, then cover with a baking tray or lid, reduce the temperature to low and cook, without stirring, for 25 minutes.

6 When cooked, fluff with a fork. Serve with yoghurt and chutney and garnish with fresh herbs and toasted cumin seeds, if desired.

TIPS: Curry leaves are available fresh or dried in many supermarkets. The fresh ones come on a small branch and can be frozen. They have a unique flavour that is hard to substitute.

I sometimes add frozen green beans to this dish for a bit of extra veg – scatter on the top after adding the stock, then fold them in at the end.

SUPER STRETCHER SPICY BEEF AND RICE

READY IN: 40 MINUTES SERVES: 4–6

250g (or more) beef mince
1 onion, finely chopped
2 cloves garlic, crushed
1½ cups basmati or jasmine rice
3 tsp beef stock powder
3¼ cups hot water
½ tsp salt
400g can of cooked lentils, drained (or pre-cook dried lentils – see tip)
a couple of handfuls of parsley, chopped

HOT SAUCE

⅓ cup sweet chilli sauce
⅓ cup tomato sauce
2 tbsp chutney
1½ tbsp Worcestershire sauce

Probably not the prettiest dish you'll ever make, but it is tasty, cheap and filling; stretching as little as 250g minced beef to serve 4 people, this recipe may just save your bacon. Serve it with some sort of vegetables, if you have any.

1 Heat a large pan and cook the mince, stirring and mashing with a masher till browned and crumbly. Add the onion and garlic and cook, stirring occasionally, until soft.

2 Combine the hot sauce ingredients and add two-thirds of the mixture to the pan. Reserve the remainder.

3 Stir in the rice, stock powder, hot water and salt, and simmer, stirring occasionally, until the rice is tender and the liquid has been absorbed. Stir in the lentils and taste – add the remaining hot sauce if you want a more punchy flavour. When the lentils are well combined, stir in the chopped parsley and serve.

TIP: You can also cook your own lentils: simmer 1 cup of green or brown lentils in boiling salted water for 20–30 minutes, until soft. Drain before using.

SPANISH BEEF AND RICE

READY IN: 40 MINUTES SERVES: 4-6

- 450g beef mince
- 1 tsp oil, if required
- ½ onion, chopped
- 2 cloves garlic, crushed
- 1 tsp ground cumin
- 2 tsp Mexican Seasoning (see page 66)
- 1½ cups basmati or jasmine rice
- ½ tsp salt
- 2 x 400g cans chopped tomatoes
- 1½ cups beef stock
- 3-4 cups chopped vegetables – fresh, frozen, or a mixture
- handful of chopped parsley, to garnish (optional)

As with the other dishes in this series, you can combine fresh and frozen vegetables – use what you have.

1 Heat a large frying pan, add the mince and cook, pressing with a potato masher until evenly brown and crumbled. Add a drop of oil if you need it. Mix in the onion and garlic and cook gently till soft.

2 Add the cumin and Mexican Seasoning and mix well, then stir in the rice, salt, tomatoes and stock. Bring to a simmer, stir once to ensure that it is not sticking to the bottom of the pan, cover with a lid or baking sheet and cook on low for 10 minutes.

3 Remove the cover and stir in the prepared vegetables. Bring the mixture back to a simmer, re-cover and cook on low, without stirring, for around 20 minutes or until the vegetables are cooked and the liquid is absorbed. Serve sprinkled with chopped parsley if desired.

LASAGNE SOUP WITH CHEESY GARLIC MELTS

READY IN: 45 MINUTES SERVES: 6

2 tsp olive oil
350–500g beef mince
1 onion, chopped
3–4 cloves garlic, crushed (around 1 tbsp)
1 courgette, chopped (or use another green vegetable – see tips)
1 carrot, peeled and chopped
500ml passata
400g can chopped tomatoes
2 cups beef stock
1 tsp extra beef stock powder
¼ cup tomato paste (around 4 tbsp)
2 tbsp chopped fresh parsley
2 tsp dried basil
1 tsp dried oregano
2 cups broken-up lasagne sheets, the crinkly kind, or other pasta such as macaroni

CHEESY GARLIC MELTS

2 tbsp butter
½ tbsp olive oil
2 cloves garlic, crushed
2 tbsp finely chopped parsley
8 slices white bread
4 slices cheese – cheddar, Edam (whatever you have)
⅓ cup grated mozzarella (optional)

TOPPING

⅓ cup ricotta
1–2 tbsp grated Parmesan
1 tbsp chopped parsley, plus extra to garnish
2 tbsp chopped basil (optional)

This hearty soup is a proper hug in a mug. The ricotta and Parmesan topping really fulfils the 'lasagne' promise, but if you don't want to bother you can just top it with grated cheese and it'll still be a winner. The super-cheesy garlicky toasties are a good addition to any tomatoey soup – or just eat them on their own!

1 Heat the oil in a large saucepan. Add the mince and cook, stirring and pressing with a fork or masher to break up any lumps. When crumbly and browned, add the onion, garlic, courgette and carrot to the pan and cook gently, stirring occasionally, until the onion is soft.

2 Add all the remaining soup ingredients except the lasagne. Bring just to the boil and simmer the soup for 30 minutes.

3 Add the uncooked lasagne directly to the soup, simmer for 10 minutes until cooked, then add some extra water to thin.

4 Make the cheesy garlic melts. Combine the butter, oil and garlic in a small microwave-safe bowl and melt in the microwave (or melt in a small saucepan). Add the chopped parsley, then brush over one side of each piece of bread. Place the cheese on the uncoated sides of 4 slices, then top with the remaining bread, with the buttery sides on the outsides. Heat the remaining butter mixture in a frying pan and gently cook the sandwiches on both sides till golden and the cheese has melted. Slice into quarters to serve.

5 Make the topping, if using, by mixing all the ingredients together. Serve the soup topped with a dollop of the ricotta mixture and a sprinkle of chopped parsley, with a cheesy melt on the side for dunking.

TIPS: Mix and match the vegetables according to what you have: capsicum, finely shredded spinach, broccoli . . .

If your jar of passata is a bit larger, just use it all – a little more won't hurt.

EASY MEATBALL LAKSA

READY IN: 30 MINUTES   SERVES: 4

½ tbsp vegetable oil
2 tbsp red curry paste
1 tbsp ground coriander
400ml can coconut milk
2 cups chicken stock – a liquid one if possible (see tips)
½ tbsp fish sauce
1 Makrut lime leaf
400g noodles
juice of 1 lime (optional)

MEATBALLS

2 slices bread
500g pork or chicken mince
2 tbsp finely chopped lemongrass, or use paste
⅓ cup sweet chilli sauce
3 tbsp soy sauce
pinch of dried chilli flakes
½ cup chopped coriander, or use paste
pinch of salt

GARNISH – OPTIONAL

chopped coriander, lime wedges, sliced chillies

My original destitute gourmet chicken laksa still has many devotees, but I've moved on and this is now my favourite. Makrut lime leaves freeze well and curry paste will keep in the fridge for ages, so once you have them in stock this dish can easily be part of your regular rotation.

1 Heat the oil in a saucepan and add the curry paste. Cook gently, stirring, for a minute, add the ground coriander, then mix in the coconut milk, stock and fish sauce. Bring to a gentle simmer and add the Makrut lime leaf.

2 Make the bread into breadcrumbs, either in a processor or with a grater over a bowl. Add the remaining meatball ingredients and pulse or mix well.

3 Scoop teaspoons of the mince mixture and form into balls with wet hands, then drop the balls gently into the simmering soup. Simmer for 7 minutes, or until the meatballs are cooked through.

4 While the meatballs cook, prepare the noodles according to the packet directions. Divide into bowls and top with the meatballs and soup. Add a squeeze of lime juice, and top with garnishes if using.

TIPS: I also use Makrut lime leaves in the Siam chicken recipe on page 54. And red curry paste is needed for the cauliflower peanut curry on page 76.

The stock is the base for the soup, so the better the stock, the better the soup in this instance. However, if you only have powder, make it anyway – then you can decide for yourself if you think it needs a liquid stock next time.

FAN FAVE

MEXICAN SPICED TOMATO SOUP (AKA MEXICAN LENTIL SOUP)

READY IN: 50 MINUTES SERVES: 4–6 AS A MEAL WITH CHEESY SCONES (SEE PAGE 116)

2 tbsp olive oil
2 onions, chopped
3 cloves garlic, crushed
3 tsp Mexican Seasoning (see below)
2 x 400g cans chopped tomatoes
1½ cups uncooked red lentils, rinsed
6 cups beef stock (see tips for vegetarian options)
⅓ cup tomato paste
2 tbsp brown sugar
½ cup chopped fresh coriander or parsley, to serve
sour cream, to serve (optional)

MEXICAN SEASONING

I use this seasoning in lots of recipes. Simply measure into an airtight container or jar, shake well and store with your spices.

1 heaped tbsp ground cumin
1 tbsp ground chilli
2 tsp sugar
1 tsp dried oregano
1 tsp salt

This dish is a serious fan favourite. Sometimes referred to as Mexican Lentil Soup, it's filling, nourishing and really savoury. Red lentils are a good source of protein, iron and fibre and contain no fat; they also cook quickly, giving this soup a thick, satisfying, hearty character in a relatively short time. It's good with some sort of cheesy bread or scone for dunking.

1 In a large saucepan, heat the oil, then add the onion and garlic and cook, stirring, until soft.

2 Stir in the Mexican Seasoning, tomatoes, lentils, stock and tomato paste, and bring to a simmer.

3 Stir in the sugar and simmer, stirring from time to time, for 45 minutes, till the soup is thick and the lentils are tender.

4 Serve topped with a dollop of sour cream (if using) and a sprinkle of the fresh herbs.

TIPS: To make this vegetarian, swap the beef stock for vegetable stock, and add a dash of soy sauce or a spoonful of miso for a hit of umami savoury flavour.

You can make this in the slow cooker; it's a bit blander – that's slow cookers for you – but there are some days when you just don't care. Prepare the recipe to the end of step 1. Reduce the stock by 1 cup. Place all the ingredients except the fresh herbs and sour cream in the slow cooker and cook on HIGH for around 6 hours or LOW for 8 hours. Season, and add a dollop more tomato paste if needed. Serve with chopped fresh herbs and sour cream as usual.

LAZY MUMMIES TRAY-BAKED PANCAKES

READY IN: 25 MINUTES SERVES: 4

1¾ cups plain flour
⅓ cup sugar
2 tsp baking powder
2 eggs
1–1¼ cups milk, soured with a squeeze of lemon juice (use as much as is needed)
1 tsp vanilla essence
2 bananas, mashed (optional)
50g butter, melted
½ cup blueberries (optional)

Cooking pancakes this way means that everyone eats together – no fuss, no juggling spatulas and multiple pans, just delicious pancakes with no hassle. Add whatever flavours or fruits you like. My Mock Maple Syrup (see the recipe below) can be made ahead of time.

1 Preheat the oven to 200°C. Place the flour, sugar and baking powder in a mixing bowl and stir together.

2 Make a well in the centre and break in the eggs. Add half the milk and use a whisk to mix, gradually incorporating the flour from around the sides of the bowl. Mix in the vanilla, and the banana if using.

3 Add the remainder of the milk in increments until you have a smooth batter. Stir in half of the melted butter, then fold in the blueberries if using.

4 Brush melted butter over the base and sides of a Swiss roll tin. Pour the batter in and dab with the remaining melted butter. Brush lightly to distribute.

5 Bake for 10 minutes until risen and set, then pop under the grill for around 2 minutes until golden on top.

6 Serve with the mock maple syrup or your favourite pancake topping or syrup.

MOCK MAPLE SYRUP
1 cup brown sugar
½ cup water
1 tsp vanilla essence

MOCK MAPLE SYRUP

READY IN: 5 MINUTES MAKES: APPROX. 300ML

1 Combine the ingredients in a small saucepan and heat until the sugar is dissolved. Store in a bottle in the fridge.

TIP: The syrup will keep for ages in the fridge. If you want to serve it warm, heat it gently in a saucepan or the microwave.

ONE-PAN CRUMPETS

READY IN: 45 MINUTES   SERVES: 4

700ml milk
2½ cups plain flour
1½ tsp salt
2 tsp sugar
½ tsp baking soda
1½ sachets instant yeast
50g butter
extra butter, to serve
honey, golden syrup or your preferred crumpet toppings

Regular-sized crumpets are a real performance to make – fiddly little greased rings in a hot pan is a sure-fire recipe for burned fingers. My One-pan Crumpets are way easier to cook, and they're a fun thing to make with the kids on a wet winter weekend. I use a frying pan or skillet about 20cm in diameter.

1 Place the milk in a saucepan to warm gently, then set aside. In a large bowl, combine the flour, salt, sugar, baking soda and yeast.

2 Gradually whisk in the warm milk; at this stage the mixture should resemble thick cream. Cover and set in a warm place for 25–30 minutes or until bubbly and risen.

3 Preheat the grill. Place an ovenproof frying pan on the stove and add the butter. When the butter is melted and foaming, use a ladle or jug to pour in a quarter of the batter, tilting the pan so that the batter covers the base.

4 Cook gently for around 5 minutes. When the surface is covered in small tubular air-holes and looks set, and the bottom – when you sneak a look underneath – is golden, place the pan under the hot grill to toast the top.

5 When lightly toasted, spread with butter and honey (or your preferred spread), cut into segments and serve while warm. Cook the remaining batter in the same manner.

TIP: You can make these ahead and freeze them, then simply reheat by toasting under the grill.

MEATLESS MEALS

A meat-free diet can be healthier and significantly cheaper than one that relies on meat, but even just introducing a couple of meatless meals into the mix each week can make a significant difference to both your budget and your health.

It's important to note that meat-free doesn't equal vegetarian. Sauces like Worcestershire sauce and fish sauce contain animal products – which is fine for flexitarians like me, but not vegetarians or vegans. You can 'veganise' many recipes by swapping milk for plant milks, cheese for vegan cheese and eggs for chia eggs (see page 91) or aquafaba (chickpea brine), but only a few of the recipes here will be suitable for vegans, as they're intended as meat-free dishes that hopefully even meat-eaters will enjoy. Most can be made vegetarian-friendly with some simple swaps if they're not already vegetarian.

POSH CAULIFLOWER CHEESE PIE

READY IN: 1 HOUR SERVES: 6

1 medium-sized head of cauliflower (about 900g)
600ml milk
50g butter
50g plain flour
1 tsp wholegrain mustard
pinch of nutmeg
150g cheese, grated
170g jar of marinated artichoke hearts, drained and chopped (optional)
salt and pepper
400g block of frozen puff pastry, defrosted
½ cup grated mozzarella (optional)
1 egg, beaten with a splash of water (egg wash)

Old-school comfort food, cauliflower cheese, is even better when baked in a crispy crust. If possible, use a dish made from metal, such as enamel or tin, as these conduct the heat efficiently and reduce the risk of a soggy bottom. I like this method for making a cheese sauce – it's quick, easy and makes a lovely thick sauce without fuss.

1 Preheat the oven to 190°C. Grease an ovenproof dish or enamel pan approx. 26cm x 21cm.

2 Rinse the cauliflower but don't remove the leaves. Trim the stalk, slice an X into the stalk end and place in a microwave-safe bowl. Add ¼ cup of water, cover and microwave for 9–12 minutes, until tender. Break into florets and coarsely chop the leaves and stem, discarding any tough parts.

3 Place the milk in a medium-sized saucepan, add the butter and heat. When the butter is beginning to melt, add the flour and whisk briskly. Continue heating and whisking until almost simmering, then cook (still whisking) for 2 minutes until thick. Remove from heat and stir in the mustard, nutmeg and cheese, and add the cauliflower, leaves and artichokes if using. Season, then set aside to cool.

4 Divide the pastry into slightly unequal halves. On a floured bench, roll out the larger portion so that it lines the dish with a 1-2cm overhang.

5 Pour in the filling, scatter with mozzarella, then roll and cover with remaining pastry, trimming so overhanging edges match. Roll overhang upwards onto rim and crimp. Brush with egg wash, cut several vents into the pastry, and bake for 35–40 minutes, until dark golden.

TIPS: Microwaving prevents the cauli becoming waterlogged, which would make the sauce watery. It's a useful technique for other cauliflower dishes, too.

If you don't want to make a pie, you can serve the filling with a topping of herby crunchy croutons made from 3 cups of cubed supermarket baguette tossed with 3 tablespoons of olive oil and ½ teaspoon of dried Italian herbs, baked at 200°C for 10–15 minutes till golden and crispy.

YUM

CAULIFLOWER, CHICKPEA AND PEANUT CURRY

READY IN: 35 MINUTES SERVES: 6

- 1 medium-sized head of cauliflower (about 900g)
- 1 tbsp oil
- 1 onion, chopped
- 2 cloves garlic, crushed
- 1 tbsp grated fresh ginger
- 1 tbsp finely chopped lemongrass, or use paste
- 2 tbsp red curry paste
- 400ml can coconut milk
- 1 tsp ground turmeric
- 1 tbsp brown sugar
- 2 tbsp soy sauce
- 1 tbsp tomato paste
- 1 tbsp fish sauce (see tip for vegetarian alternatives)
- ⅓ cup crunchy peanut butter
- 400g can chickpeas, rinsed and drained
- handful of chopped coriander or a dollop of coriander paste
- cooked rice, for serving
- handful each of chopped coriander and peanuts, to garnish (optional)

I originally developed this recipe for a Love Food Hate Waste campaign, as it's a good recipe for using the whole cauli – florets, leaves and stem. Since then I've made it many times both with and without meat.

1 Remove the leaves and stalk from the cauliflower. Rinse and slice the leaves. Cut the stalk longwise and then slice thinly. Separate the head into florets and set aside.

2 Heat the oil in a large frying pan over medium heat. Add the onion, garlic, ginger, lemongrass and sliced cauliflower leaves and stalk, and cook, stirring occasionally, until the onion is soft. Add the curry paste and cook for another minute, stirring frequently.

3 Add the coconut milk, turmeric, sugar, soy sauce, tomato paste, fish sauce and peanut butter. Stir, heating gently until simmering.

4 Add the cauliflower florets and cover, cooking for 5–10 minutes until the cauliflower is tender but not mushy. Stir in the chickpeas and coriander and season with salt.

5 Remove the cover and simmer until thickened. Serve with rice and a sprinkling of chopped coriander and chopped peanuts if desired.

TIP: To make this vegetarian-friendly, you can make a fish sauce substitute from soy sauce, miso paste, dried mushrooms, sugar and dried seaweed – there are lots of recipes online. I would opt for a dollop of miso paste myself. Miso keeps in the fridge indefinitely, so won't go to waste.

EASY SPINACH AND RICOTTA PASTA BAKE

READY IN: 50 MINUTES SERVES: 6

500g ricotta
2 cloves garlic, crushed
½ tsp chilli flakes
100g feta, crumbled
250g fresh or frozen spinach, or silver beet or a mixture, rinsed, chopped and squeezed
2 tbsp chopped parsley
2 tbsp chopped basil (or use basil pesto or basil paste from a tube)
½ cup grated Parmesan
salt and pepper
700g passata
3 large fresh or 8–12 dried lasagne sheets, depending on the size of your dish
1 cup grated cheese

I've made this dish using fresh spinach, fresh silver beet, frozen spinach and a mix of all three. I've even made it with home-made ricotta and never been disappointed. You can freeze ricotta if you find it on special in the supermarket, or sub it out for cottage cheese. See page 105 for how to make a cheat's home-made ricotta.

1 Preheat the oven to 190°C. Grease an approx. 28cm x 20cm lasagne dish.

2 In a large bowl, combine the ricotta, garlic, chilli flakes, feta, spinach, parsley, basil and half the Parmesan. Season with salt and pepper and mix well.

3 Spread one-third of the passata in the bottom of the dish and place a layer of lasagne sheets over the top. Using a fork, spread the lasagne with half the ricotta-spinach mixture. Cover with another layer of pasta, another third of the passata, and then the remaining ricotta-spinach mixture.

4 Place a final layer of pasta over the ricotta-spinach mixture. Cover with the final third of the passata and scatter on the remaining Parmesan and grated cheese. Bake for 35–40 minutes, or until golden and bubbling.

TIP: While ricotta, feta and Parmesan are not inexpensive, this pasta bake is a much quicker and cheaper option than a traditional lasagne. Spinach and silver beet are both really easy to grow, too.

ROSEMARY ROASTED VEGETABLE STRUDEL

READY IN: 1 HOUR SERVES: 6

- approx. 500g roasting vegetables (such as kumara, pumpkin, beetroot, butternut . . .), peeled and cut into approx. 1½ cm pieces
- ¼ cup olive oil
- 1 sprig of rosemary, plus an additional ½ tbsp finely chopped
- 300g mushrooms, sliced
- 1 onion, chopped
- 2 cloves garlic, crushed
- ½ tsp dried sage
- 2 slices bread, made into breadcrumbs
- ¼ cup ground almonds
- 2 tbsp pine nuts
- 1 egg, lightly beaten
- salt and pepper
- 8 sheets of filo pastry

The filling for this dish can also be used to make individual rolls – divide the mixture into 'sausages' of your desired size and roll in a sheet of puff pastry. Cut into sections, brush with beaten egg and bake.

1 Preheat the oven to 220°C. If using beetroot, place it in a shallow roasting pan with ½ tablespoon of the oil, toss to coat and roast for 15 minutes. Add the remaining vegetables, rosemary sprig and a drop more oil if needed. Toss to coat and roast for 20–25 minutes or until tender.

2 While the vegetables are cooking, heat another ½ tablespoon of oil in a frying pan and cook the mushrooms, onion and garlic gently, stirring occasionally, till tender. Remove from the heat. Mix in the chopped rosemary, sage, breadcrumbs, ground almonds and pine nuts. When cool, add the egg and mix together, then fold in the roasted vegetables (discarding the rosemary sprig). Season with salt and pepper.

3 Brush a sheet of filo pastry with oil and lay another on top, brush with oil and lay on another. Continue till you have a stack of 8 sheets.

4 With the long edge of the filo facing you, scoop the filling mixture into a log shape along the nearest edge. Leave 2cm of uncovered filo pastry at each end.

5 Gently fold the pastry end edges inwards and then roll the strudel into a neat parcel with the join on the bottom. Slip it onto a greased baking sheet and brush lightly with oil. Bake for 25–30 minutes, or until golden. Serve in slices with chutney or tomato relish.

TIPS: Keep the unused filo covered with a damp tea towel while you are working, to prevent it drying out.

Make fresh breadcrumbs by grating bread on the coarse side of a grater if you don't have a processor.

LOADED QUINOA CHILLI NACHOS

READY IN: 45 MINUTES SERVES: 4

½ tbsp oil
1 onion, chopped
2 cloves garlic, crushed
2½ tsp Mexican Seasoning (see page 66)
½ tsp smoked paprika
400g can chopped tomatoes
500g pumpkin, kumara or butternut, peeled and chopped into roughly 1cm pieces
¾ cup quinoa, uncooked
2 cups vegetable stock
2 tbsp tomato paste
425g can chilli beans in sauce (I use the 'hot' ones)

TO SERVE

300g bag of corn chips (I use spicy ones)
1½ cups grated pizza cheese, or your preferred cheese (vegan if desired)
250g chopped tomatoes or cherry tomatoes
2 tbsp pumpkin seeds, toasted and salted (see tips)
½ cup sour cream, mixed with a squeeze of lime juice (optional)

CHUNKY GUACAMOLE – OPTIONAL

1 avocado, halved and deseeded
¼ red onion, chopped
handful of coriander, chopped
a good squeeze of lime or lemon juice

You could serve this chilli over rice or in a buddha bowl with toppings if you don't want to do the cheesy corn-chips thing. Hard-core chilli eaters can ramp up the heat by adding more of the Mexican Seasoning or adding a scattering of sliced fresh chilli or dried chilli flakes before serving.

1 In a large frying pan, heat the oil. Add the onion and garlic and cook until tender.

2 Add the spices, then stir in the chopped tomatoes, pumpkin, quinoa and stock and bring to a simmer. Mix in the tomato paste and chilli beans in sauce, then cover and simmer gently, stirring frequently, until the pumpkin is tender, the liquid has been absorbed and the quinoa is plump.

3 If making the guacamole, mash the avocado in a bowl and mix with remaining ingredients.

4 Preheat the grill. Arrange the corn chips on a shallow heatproof tray or individual plates, and top with quinoa chilli and a generous sprinkle of grated cheese. Grill until the cheese is melted.

5 Scatter with chopped tomatoes and toasted pumpkin seeds. Serve with sour cream and guacamole if desired.

TIPS: To toast pumpkin seeds, place in a pan with a drop of oil and fry over medium heat, turning once or twice, till golden.

You could roast the pumpkin in the oven while the quinoa cooks (without a lid) and stir it in at the end, or use leftover roast veg if you prefer the sweeter flavour produced by roasting.

Want more veg? Add chopped celery and capsicum to the onion and garlic at the start, and serve with a salad or slaw.

PUMPKIN AND RICOTTA CALZONES

READY IN: 1 HOUR   MAKES: 8

DOUGH

3 cups plain flour
1 tbsp sugar
1 tsp salt
3 tbsp olive oil
1 sachet instant yeast
1–1½ cups warm water

FILLING

a big wedge of pumpkin – enough to make 2 cups when cut into 1½ cm pieces
1½ tbsp olive oil
1 onion, chopped
3 cloves garlic, crushed
120g chopped spinach
½ tsp dried sage
pinch of chilli flakes
1 egg
¼ cup grated Parmesan, plus extra for sprinkling if desired
250g ricotta, store-bought or home-made (see page 105)

These savoury calzones are rib-stickingly filling. Good hot for dinner or cold for a picnic. I serve them with a dollop of chutney or relish.

1 Make the dough. Combine the flour, sugar, salt, oil and yeast in a large bowl, then mix with enough warm water to form a dough. Knead the dough for 3–5 minutes, adding more flour if needed to prevent the dough sticking, till it is smooth and elastic.

2 Place the dough in a clean, greased bowl and cover with cling film. Microwave on **low** power for 1 minute, rest the dough for 10 minutes, then repeat. After the second rest, the dough should have doubled in size. (Alternatively, set aside in a warm place until doubled in size, about 40 minutes.)

3 While the dough is rising, prepare the filling. Preheat the oven to 220°C. Spread the pumpkin on a greased baking tray and toss with ½ tablespoon of the oil. Roast for 15–20 minutes until tender, then leave to cool.

4 Heat a drop of the oil in a frying pan, add the onion and garlic and cook gently, stirring occasionally, until soft. Add the chopped spinach and seasonings and set aside. When cool, mix in the cooked pumpkin, egg, Parmesan and ricotta. Reduce the oven to 200°C.

5 Divide the dough into 8 pieces. Roll on a floured bench into 18cm circles. Divide the filling mixture into eight and place a portion on half of each circle, leaving a 2cm border. Fold and pinch to close. Place on a greased baking tray. Cut vents in the tops and bake for 8 minutes. Brush the tops with oil, add a sprinkle of Parmesan if desired, and bake for another 8 minutes.

TIP: These can also be frozen. After defrosting, reheat in the oven to crisp up the crust.

MUSHROOM, PECAN AND CARAMELISED ONION WELLINGTON

READY IN: 1 HOUR 40 MINUTES SERVES: 6

- 2 large onions, thinly sliced
- 2 tbsp olive oil
- 1 tbsp brown sugar
- 3 cloves garlic, crushed
- 500g mushrooms, chopped coarsely or pulsed in a processor
- 2 tbsp brandy
- pinch of thyme
- 1 large sprig of rosemary, chopped
- 3 slices bread, made into breadcrumbs
- ½ cup pecans, lightly toasted then finely chopped
- 1 tbsp soy sauce
- 1 apple, grated
- 2 eggs, lightly beaten (keep them separate)
- salt and pepper
- 400g block puff pastry, defrosted
- 1 quantity of Marvellous Meat-free Gravy (see page 125)

This dish is easily good enough for a celebration meal. Do allow the pastry to cook completely – not just golden but a rich dark golden, as it can be quite thick on the ends. In the rush of cooking dishes to photograph for this book, I undercooked the one pictured. It was too late to reshoot it, but I slung it back in the oven afterwards and it was delicious!

1 Make the caramelised onions. Cook the onions in 1 tablespoon of the oil in a saucepan, stirring frequently till dark golden. Stir in the sugar and cook till caramel-coloured.

2 While the onions are cooking, preheat the oven to 200°C and prepare the filling. In a frying pan, heat the remaining oil. Add the garlic and mushrooms and cook, stirring frequently, until beginning to soften. Stir in the brandy and herbs, then add the breadcrumbs, chopped pecans and soy sauce.

3 Stir in the apple, remove from the heat, mix well and allow to cool. When cooled, add one beaten egg and season well with salt and pepper. (Reserve remaining egg to glaze the pastry.)

4 Roll out the pastry on a floured bench to roughly 35cm long and 25cm wide. Brush the edges with beaten egg. Arrange the mushroom filling in a loaf shape down the middle. Top with caramelised onions. Fold in the short ends of the pastry, then wrap over the long sides to overlap and enclose the filling. Carefully, flip join-side-down onto a greased tray.

5 Using a serrated knife, lightly score diagonal lines in the pastry, then brush all over with beaten egg. Bake for 40–45 minutes, or until the pastry is a rich golden colour.

6 Make the meat-free gravy to serve.

TIP: To make this vegan-friendly, use a vegan pastry and swap the egg in the filling for a chia egg (see page 91). Use soy milk to glaze the pastry and replace the butter in the gravy with olive oil or a dairy-free spread.

SELF-CRUSTING QUICHE

READY IN: 45 MINUTES SERVES: 4–6

- 1 tbsp oil or butter
- 1 large onion, chopped
- 2 cloves garlic, crushed
- ½ cup self-raising flour
- 3 eggs
- 1 cup milk
- seasoning: salt and pepper, plus dried or fresh herbs, Mexican Seasoning (see page 66), Parmesan cheese, and a dash of sweet chilli sauce, pesto or curry powder . . .
- 2 potatoes, scrubbed, cooked and cubed
- 1 cup cooked vegetables, canned corn or roast pumpkin, steamed mixed veg, peas . . .
- 1 cup grated cheese
- sauce, salsa or chutney to serve (optional)

This dish has been a fan fave from the beginning. It's something of a cross between a frittata and a quiche, and it's really versatile. You can make it cheesy, or spicy, meatless or loaded – pretty much however you want it. The cup of cooked veggies can be roasted, steamed or boiled, so just use this a base formula and tweak to suit what's in your fridge. The one in the photo had roasted veggies and cheese, which went really well with a drizzle of sweet chilli sauce.

1 Preheat the oven to 220°C. Grease a 24cm baking dish or pie plate.

2 Heat the oil or butter in a small pan and add the onion and garlic. Cook gently, stirring occasionally, till soft, then remove from the heat and leave to cool.

3 Place the flour in a large bowl and set aside. In a separate bowl, combine the eggs, milk and seasonings of your choice, including salt and pepper. Whisk with a fork, then pour over the flour and stir until just combined.

4 Add the prepared vegetables and anything else you are including, then fold in the grated cheese. Pour into the dish and bake for 30 minutes, till puffed, golden and cooked. Cool for 5 minutes before cutting. Serve hot or cold.

TIP: Great for making use of leftovers such as chilli or a cold sausage or two, or add some sliced salami or cooked bacon.

VEGETABLE SHEPHERD'S PIE WITH SWEET KUMARA TOPPING

READY IN: 1 HOUR 10 MINUTES SERVES: 6

1 tbsp oil
1 onion, chopped
4 cloves garlic, minced
2 carrots, peeled and chopped
1 stalk celery, chopped
400g mushrooms, sliced
2 tsp dried thyme
200ml red wine (possibly sloshed out of the cook's glass)
1½ tbsp plain flour
2 cups vegetable stock
2 x 400g cans lentils, drained
2 tbsp soy sauce
⅓ cup store-bought BBQ sauce
1 cup frozen peas

KUMARA TOPPING

1kg kumara, peeled and cut into chunks
2 tbsp butter
½ cup milk
salt and pepper

This meatless pie is a bit more sophisticated than many, thanks to the red wine, which adds a layer of complexity to the flavour. If you don't have or prefer not to use alcohol, you could add 200ml of dried-mushroom soaking water and maybe a drop of lemon juice to replace the acidity.

1 Heat the oil in a large frying pan. Add the onion, garlic, carrots and celery and cook gently, stirring occasionally, for 4–5 minutes, until becoming tender. Add the mushrooms and thyme and cook gently for another few minutes until softened.

2 Add the wine and simmer until evaporated. Stir in the flour, then gradually mix in the stock a little at a time to make a lump-free sauce. Add the lentils and simmer for 25–30 minutes, until the sauce has thickened. Preheat the oven to 220°C.

3 Prepare the topping. Steam or boil the kumara till tender. Drain, add the butter, and mash, adding milk as needed to achieve a soft, spreadable consistency. Season with salt and pepper.

4 To the vegetable and lentil mixture, add the soy sauce, BBQ sauce and peas. Transfer to a casserole dish. Top with mashed kumara and bake for 15–20 minutes, until the pie is bubbling and the topping is crisp.

TIP: You could swap the kumara for a cheesy potato mash or cook the filling and use it for pies or pot pies.

VEGETARIAN/VEGAN SPICY 'MEATBALLS'

READY IN: 40 MINUTES SERVES: 4–6

- 1 tbsp olive oil
- 1½ cups mushrooms, coarsely chopped
- 1 onion, chopped
- 3 cloves garlic, crushed
- 1½ tbsp Mexican Seasoning (see page 66), or other seasoning such as Italian herbs, curry powder, Moroccan seasoning . . .
- ½ tsp salt
- 2 cups cubed roasted kumara or pumpkin
- 1 cup rolled oats
- ½ cup cooked brown rice
- 1 egg or chia egg (see tips)
- 1 tbsp soy sauce
- 1 tbsp tomato sauce
- 1 extra tsp oil

This is a good, tasty meatless meatball method to use in place of regular meatballs in many recipes. You can free-flow freeze them, too, for a meatless meal option at short notice. Roast extra kumara or pumpkin next time so you can make a batch.

1 Preheat the oven to 180°C. In a large frying pan, heat the olive oil and gently cook the mushrooms till soft.

2 Add the onion and garlic, and when soft mix in the Mexican Seasoning or seasoning of your choice. Cook for 2 minutes, stirring occasionally, then place the mixture in a processor together with all the remaining ingredients except the oil. Pulse until mixed but still a bit chunky.

3 Roll into balls with wet hands. Heat the remaining oil in a shallow roasting pan, roll the balls in the oil and bake, shaking the pan from time to time, until browned, around 20 minutes.

TIPS: If money-saving is not a consideration, you can buy microwaveable sachets or pottles of brown rice already cooked. If you do want to keep the cost down, cook a batch of brown rice and freeze in resealable bags to use as needed.

To make a chia egg, mix 1 tablespoon of chia seeds with 2½ tablespoons of water and let sit for 3 minutes.

SNACKS, SALADS, SIDES AND SAUCES

When we hit the supermarket to do a shop, it's often the little things that catch us out at the checkout – that impulse decision to grab some chips and dips or a few bits and bobs from the deli or freezers to have on hand 'in case' friends pop over or the house is overrun with hungry kids.

Happily, that spur-of-the-moment socialising doesn't have to blow your budget. The following recipes include some easy ideas for things that can be served as nibbles or combined to create sharing platters for spontaneous gatherings, along with some useful cheats and techniques to help you avoid the always-expensive emergency dash to the supermarket.

MAHARAJA PIES

READY IN: 1¼ HOURS INCLUDING MARINATING MAKES: 16

juice of 1 lemon
1 tsp grated ginger
2 skinless, boneless chicken breasts, cut into small pieces
1 tbsp oil
1 tbsp curry powder
1 tsp ground cumin
1 tsp ground coriander
¼ tsp ground chilli
⅓ cup tomato paste
¼ cup plain flour
1 cup chicken stock
1 tbsp brown sugar
splash of cream
1 tbsp cornflour mixed with 1 tbsp cold water, if needed
4 sheets puff pastry, defrosted
¼ cup milk
½ tbsp poppy seeds
Minty Yoghurt Sauce (page 27) or chutney, to serve (optional)

This recipe was my kids' idea, as they were obsessed with an Indian spiced chicken pie sold through a fast-food chain. I was persuaded to come up with a home-made version of their favourite take-out treat, and here it is.

1 In a non-reactive bowl, combine the lemon juice and ginger, add the chicken and stir to coat. Set aside to marinate for 10 minutes.

2 Heat the oil in a frying pan and cook the chicken until sealed all over. Add the spices, tomato paste and flour and stir to mix, then stir in the chicken stock to make a gravy. Add the sugar and simmer for 10 minutes. Stir in the cream. If the sauce hasn't reduced and thickened, stir in the cornflour mixture – but only if needed.

3 Preheat the oven to 210°C. Divide the pastry sheets into quarters. Brush the edges very lightly with water. Take one square of pastry and bring opposing corners together. Pinch to join them, then add a third corner, pinching the edges together to form a pocket. Spoon filling into the pocket, then bring the remaining corner to the centre and pinch along the edges to seal in the filling. Place on a lightly greased baking tray.

4 Repeat with all the remaining squares of pastry. Brush the pies lightly with milk and sprinkle with poppy seeds. Bake for 20–25 minutes, or until golden and crisp. Serve with Minty Yoghurt Sauce or chutney.

TIP: I use this technique for making sweet and savoury hand pies. It's a great way to make a little bit go a long way.

CURRIED CHICKEN SALAD IN LETTUCE CUPS WITH QUICK PICKLED VEGETABLES

READY IN: 35 MINUTES SERVES: 4 AS A SNACK

⅓ cup mayonnaise
⅓ cup natural unsweetened yoghurt
1 tbsp red curry paste
2 tbsp mango chutney
1 tbsp fresh lemon juice
salt and pepper
350–400g (2 medium-sized) chicken breasts, cooked and chopped
¼ cup chopped chives, spring onion or red onion
2 large stalks celery, chopped
1 cup chopped cucumber
½ cup chopped colourful capsicum
8 iceberg lettuce leaves
handful of chopped parsley or coriander
1 cup chopped mixed-colour cherry tomatoes (optional)

QUICK PICKLED VEGETABLES

½ cup white vinegar
¼ cup sugar
⅛ tsp salt
2 medium-sized carrots, julienned
½ red onion, cut into thin slices

This tasty, tangy combo is great for a light meal or lunch, or you could shred the lettuce and use it to fill crispy tortilla bowls. The quick pickle is also good tucked into a burger.

1 Make the pickled vegetables. Combine the vinegar, sugar and salt in a non-reactive bowl and whisk till the sugar has dissolved. Immerse the carrot and onion in the brine and marinate for 30 minutes. Strain and reserve brine – store in the fridge for next time.

2 In a large bowl, whisk together the mayonnaise, yoghurt, curry paste, mango chutney and lemon juice. Season with salt and pepper, then add the chicken, chives/onion, celery, cucumber and capsicum and stir gently to combine.

3 Layer two lettuce leaves together to form a bowl, and divide the salad between the lettuce bowls. Top with chopped herbs and cherry tomatoes if desired.

TIP: Try this salad in a crispy tortilla cup instead, or roll it up in flatbread and pack for lunch.

CRUNCHY SPICY CHICKEN NIBBLES WITH ALABAMA DIPPING SAUCE

READY IN: 50 MINUTES   SERVES: 4–6 AS A SNACK

150g spicy corn chips
1 cup panko breadcrumbs
2 tsp Mexican Seasoning (see page 66)
½ tsp ground chilli
½ tsp dried oregano
½ tsp salt
1kg chicken nibbles (approx. 24)
2 eggs, lightly beaten
cooking spray

ALABAMA DIPPING SAUCE

1 cup mayonnaise
⅛ cup cider vinegar
1 tbsp Dijon mustard
2 tsp 'cream style' horseradish (available in the supermarket)
1 clove garlic, crushed
¼ tsp paprika
handful of fresh basil leaves, finely chopped
salt and pepper

I don't realistically expect most households to have both Dijon mustard and a jar of horseradish just hanging around – however, if you buy these to make this sauce, you will not regret it. I think it's the kind of thing that a famous burger chain may have originally based their sauce on, so not surprisingly it's pretty addictive smeared on sandwiches and burgers or as a dip for just about anything savoury.

1 Preheat the oven to 190°C. Place the corn chips in a processor or sturdy bag, and pulse or crush to form crumbs. Add the breadcrumbs, seasonings and salt and pulse or shake bag to mix. Pour into a bowl.

2 Dunk the chicken nibbles in the beaten egg, then coat in the crumb mix. Arrange on a baking tray lined with non-stick baking paper, and spray generously with cooking spray. Bake for 35 minutes, or till golden.

3 Make the Alabama Dipping Sauce. In a medium-sized bowl, whisk all of the ingredients together until smooth. Transfer to a jar with a tight lid and refrigerate until needed (up to a week).

TIP: You can use the crunchy crumb mixture for home-made chicken nuggets or even for crumbing fish.

PORK & CABBAGE SPRING ROLLS WITH PEANUT PINEAPPLE DIPPING SAUCE

READY IN: 45 MINUTES PLUS COOLING
MAKES: 18–20 FRIED ROLLS OR 20–30 RICE WRAPPER ROLLS

⅓ cup dried shiitake mushrooms
1 cup boiling water
1 tsp sesame oil
250g pork mince
1 clove garlic, minced
2 medium-sized carrots, finely sliced or grated (about 1 cup)
1 cup water chestnuts, coarsely chopped
6 cups (around 350g) finely sliced green cabbage
2 tbsp Shaoxing wine (Chinese rice wine)
3 tbsp hoisin sauce
¼ cup soy sauce
1 tbsp oyster sauce
salt and pepper
2 tbsp cornflour mixed with 2 tbsp cold water

FOR FRIED SPRING ROLLS

18–20 square spring roll wrappers, approx. 20cm
canola oil for frying

FOR SUMMER ROLLS

1 cup fresh herb leaves – mint or coriander
20–30 rice paper wrappers

PEANUT PINEAPPLE DIPPING SAUCE

½ cup crunchy peanut butter
⅓ cup canned crushed pineapple, including juice
1 tbsp lemongrass, chopped
1 clove garlic, chopped
½ tsp chilli flakes
1 tbsp fish sauce
1½ tsp soy sauce

Buying snacks or appetisers for parties is expensive – but often the ingredients are cheap, and once you have them in stock they last a long time. This recipe gives you the option of a crispy fried spring roll or a lighter 'summer roll' wrapped in a rice wrapper. Both are really tasty , and so is the dipping sauce – try it with kebabs or satay skewers, too.

1 Soak the dried mushrooms in the boiling water.

2 Heat the oil in a frying pan and cook the pork mince until browned, breaking it up with a masher to a fine crumbly consistency. Drain the mushrooms, reserving ¼ cup of the liquid, and chop the mushrooms finely.

3 Stir the mushrooms, garlic, carrots, water chestnuts and cabbage into the mince, then add the Shaoxing wine, sauces and reserved mushroom soaking water. Cook until the liquid has evaporated, and season with salt and pepper. Thicken with half the cornflour mixture. Set aside to cool.

4 For fried spring rolls: take a wrapper, and with one corner facing you, put a dessertspoon of mixture in a line 5cm from the corner. Roll once to enclose the filling. Fold in the sides, then roll up completely and seal with a dab of the cornflour mixture. Continue till all the filling is used. Heat 5–7cm depth of oil in a saucepan and cook the spring rolls a few at a time until golden, approx. 1–2 minutes. Drain on a kitchen towel-lined plate and keep warm. Serve with sauce.

5 For 'summer' rolls: pour hot water into a shallow bowl. Soak a wrapper for 30 seconds or until soft, then place on a clean tea towel. Position a few herb leaves on to the wrapper. Top with a spoonful of filling mixture. Roll over once to enclose the filling, then tuck in the sides and continue rolling to form a neat parcel. Repeat until all the filling is used.

PEANUT PINEAPPLE DIPPING SAUCE
READY IN: 5 MINUTES MAKES: 1 CUP

1 Combine all the ingredients in a processor or blender and process till smooth. Store in the fridge for up to 3 days.

SPINACH AND WHITE BEAN CROQUETTES WITH PESTO MAYO

READY IN: 35 MINUTES MAKES: 12

- 2 tbsp olive oil
- 2 cloves garlic, crushed
- handful of fresh oregano leaves, roughly chopped
- 2 x 400g cans white beans (butter or cannellini), drained
- 100g spinach, removed from stems, finely chopped and excess moisture wrung out
- 1 tbsp white or cider vinegar
- salt and pepper
- ½ cup grated Parmesan
- ½ cup plain flour
- 1 egg, lightly beaten
- 1 cup dried breadcrumbs (preferably panko as they're the crispiest)
- 2 tbsp butter
- ⅓ cup canola oil, for frying
- 2 tbsp basil pesto (or a handful of chopped basil leaves)
- ⅔ cup aïoli

This recipe uses canned beans as a base, but mashed potatoes also make a good base for a croquette (see the next recipe). Once you've mastered the basic principles, mix and match the flavours.

1 Heat the olive oil in a frying pan, add the garlic and oregano and cook gently, stirring, for several minutes to allow the flavours to infuse. Add the beans and spinach to the pan and cook, stirring frequently, till the spinach is cooked.

2 Add the vinegar and salt and pepper, and continue to cook gently for 5–10 minutes, till the moisture has evaporated. Remove from the heat and coarsely mash the beans with a potato masher. Mix in the Parmesan, then leave until cool enough to handle.

3 Place three shallow bowls on the bench with flour in one, beaten egg in the next and breadcrumbs in the third. Divide the bean mixture into 12 even-sized balls, then roll into cylinders. Coat each cylinder first in flour, then in beaten egg and lastly in breadcrumbs.

4 Heat the butter and canola oil in a shallow pan. When shimmering, gently pan-fry the croquettes in batches till golden brown on all sides, approx. 5-7 minutes.

5 Mix the pesto and aïoli together and serve with the croquettes.

TIP: These croquettes make a great meatless meal served with a salad, as well as a delicious finger food.

CRISPY LEFTOVER CHRISTMAS HAM CROQUETTES

READY IN: 45 MINUTES PLUS CHILLING MAKES: 24

1kg floury potatoes, scrubbed
½ tbsp oil
1 onion, finely chopped
50g butter
couple of handfuls of fresh herbs, finely chopped (parsley, oregano – whatever you have)
¼ cup grated Parmesan
¼ cup finely chopped chives or spring onion
1 tbsp wholegrain mustard
salt and pepper
250–350g ham off the bone, chopped finely
¼ cup plain flour
3 eggs, lightly beaten
2 cups panko breadcrumbs
1.5 litres oil, for frying
aïoli or sauce (optional), to serve – the Alabama Dipping Sauce on page 98 goes really well with these.

Mashed potato makes a great base for croquettes, and croquettes are a great way to use up leftover Christmas ham. These are deep-fried not shallow-fried, so make sure you have enough oil.

1 Cut the potatoes into large chunks and boil in salted water until tender when pricked with a fork. Drain and return to the heat for a minute to dry out. While the potatoes are cooking, heat the oil in a small pan and cook the onion gently, stirring occasionally, till tender, then set aside.

2 Mash the potatoes with a masher and then with a fork, working in the butter until smooth. Mash in the cooked onion along with the herbs, Parmesan, chives and mustard, then season with salt and pepper. Fold in the ham, mixing well.

3 Turn the mixture out onto a board and pat into a ball. Divide in half, then divide each half into 12 pieces. Roll each piece into a neat cylinder and place on a tray. Chill in the freezer for half an hour, to firm up.

4 Place the flour, beaten eggs and breadcrumbs in three separate shallow bowls. Coat each croquette in flour, then egg, then breadcrumbs, and return to the tray. When coated, the croquettes can either be frozen or cooked straight away. If frozen, defrost before cooking.

5 Heat the oil in a deep saucepan to 180°C. (If you don't have a thermometer, stick the end of a wooden spoon into the oil. When lots of bubbles gently float up around the handle, the oil is ready. If bubbling hard, it's too hot.) Fry the croquettes two or three at a time until crisp and golden, around 4–5 minutes. Transfer to a plate lined with kitchen towels and keep warm in a low oven while you are frying the next lot. Serve with your favourite dipping sauce.

TIPS: I don't peel the spuds, as the skins more or less disappear when you mash the mixture.

When the oil is fully cold, line a sieve with a piece of kitchen towel and strain it into a jug for reuse.

CHEAT'S HOME-MADE RICOTTA

READY IN: A FEW HOURS, OR OVERNIGHT MAKES: AROUND 1¼ CUPS

2 litres full-fat milk
¼ cup white vinegar
pinch of salt

True ricotta is made from the whey left over from cheese-making. This easy home-made version using full-fat milk is an acceptable substitute for store-bought ricotta, and it costs about half the price – less if you use milk made from powder. The quantity can be doubled, but you might need to strain it in two separate sieves, as it will be a lot to handle when you get to the squeezing stage.

1 Gently heat the milk to 80°C – just under boiling – stirring frequently to prevent it sticking; a thermometer is helpful if you have one. Remove from the heat, add the vinegar and salt, and stir gently for 1 minute. Curds should begin to form immediately.

2 Cover with a clean, dry cloth and leave undisturbed for a couple of hours or overnight. Resist the temptation to poke the mixture.

3 Line a sieve with muslin or a clean linen tea towel and place it over a bowl. With a slotted spoon, ladle curds into the sieve. Leave to drain for a few hours, until firm but still creamy.

4 Twist the cloth to gently squeeze out the liquid. If the liquid is milky, you don't need to squeeze it any more. Cover the ricotta and refrigerate till required (up to 2 days only).

HONEY-BAKED HALOUMI SALAD WITH RASPBERRY BASIL VINAIGRETTE

READY IN: 20 MINUTES PLUS 15 MINUTES MARINATING SERVES: 4–6

RASPBERRY BASIL VINAIGRETTE

2 tbsp lemon or lime juice
1 tbsp balsamic vinegar
½ cup raspberries (fresh or defrosted)
1 tbsp chopped fresh basil
pinch of salt
⅛ tsp Dijon mustard
2–3 tsp honey, according to your taste
1 tbsp olive oil

SALAD

3 tbsp olive oil
2 tbsp honey
handful of oregano leaves, finely chopped
zest and juice of 1 lemon
2 cloves garlic, crushed
2 x 225g blocks of haloumi cheese, cut into thick slices
baby leaf salad for 4 people
½ telegraph cucumber, sliced into ribbons
½ cup fresh raspberries
½ cup toasted walnuts
bread, to serve

Serve as a salad, light meal or meatless main course. Haloumi has a mild, sweet flavour and an engaging squeaky texture.

1 Make the dressing. Blend the dressing ingredients in a processor or blender. Sieve to remove solids if desired. Set aside in the fridge.

2 Make the salad. In a shallow, non-reactive dish, combine the olive oil, honey, oregano, lemon juice and garlic. Coat the haloumi in the mixture and leave to marinate for 15 minutes; or keep overnight, covered, in the fridge.

3 In a frying pan or on a grill plate, cook the haloumi for 1–2 minutes on each side, till browned but not runny.

4 Arrange the salad leaves and cucumber ribbons on a serving platter or plates, and add the haloumi, raspberries and walnuts. Drizzle the haloumi with any remaining marinade. Serve the salad with Raspberry Basil Vinaigrette and good bread.

TIP: Serve as a vegetarian main course. If barbecuing, place the haloumi in a small pan on the barbecue, clear of cooking meats.

ROASTED VEGETABLE SALAD WITH CURRIED COUSCOUS

READY IN: 50 MINUTES   SERVES: 6 AS A SIDE DISH

1 potato, scrubbed
1 kumara, peeled
a wedge of pumpkin
2 carrots
1 capsicum (optional)
1 red onion, cut into wedges
2 tbsp olive oil
1 cup instant couscous
1 tsp chicken stock powder
1 cup boiling water
drained canned chickpeas (optional)

CURRIED DRESSING

2 tsp curry powder
¼ cup olive oil
2 tbsp malt, white or cider vinegar
½ tbsp sugar
1 clove garlic, crushed
fresh herbs, to garnish (optional)

This versatile salad is a fan favourite. Always popular when taken to shared-meal-type events, it also makes a good base for adding toppings such as last night's leftovers. You can include any vegetables suitable for roasting.

1 Preheat the oven to 220°C. Chop the vegetables into similar-sized pieces, around 2cm, and place with the onion wedges in a shallow roasting pan.

2 Drizzle with the oil and toss to coat, then arrange in a single layer. Cook, turning occasionally, for 30–40 minutes or until golden and cooked.

3 Place the couscous in a medium-sized heatproof bowl. Combine the stock powder and boiling water and stir into the couscous. Quickly cover with a plate or lid to retain the heat, and leave for a few minutes for the liquid to be absorbed. Fluff the couscous with a fork, then add the roasted vegetables and chickpeas if using.

4 Combine the dressing ingredients and pour into the couscous. Fold in till evenly mixed. Transfer to a serving platter and garnish with fresh herbs if desired.

TIP: This is a great way to use leftover roast veg. It's also easy to transport and pretty cheap to make all year round, so is great to take to a barbecue or picnic.

CRUSTY BRUSCHETTA WITH HERBY WHIPPED FETA

READY IN: 20 MINUTES SERVES 4

- 125g feta cheese (or other soft feta-style cheese, such as chèvre)
- 70g cream cheese
- 1 tbsp honey
- small handful of fresh basil leaves
- a couple of fresh thyme sprigs
- ½ tsp fresh oregano leaves
- 8 small slices crusty bread
- olive oil spray
- 4 slices prosciutto (or ham), halved longwise – or cherry tomatoes, or sliced seasonal fruits (see tip)
- honey, for drizzling

Make bruschetta for a pre-dinner nibble, party platter or easy informal lunch for guests. I often use my no-knead bread, as pictured (recipe on page 112), but any good crusty loaf works well.

1 Make the whipped feta. In a processor, combine the feta, cream cheese, honey and herbs, beating until smooth. If you don't have a processor, chop the herbs finely, then beat the feta till smooth, then add the cream cheese, herbs and honey and mix well.

2 Preheat the grill. Spray the bread lightly on each side with olive oil, and grill each side until lightly toasted.

3 Spread the toasted bread with whipped feta and top with a twist of prosciutto or ham. Drizzle lightly with honey before serving.

TIP: Add a slice of fruit to the bruschetta – pear, peach, fig or persimmon, when in season. Or swap the whipped feta for the pea pesto on page 113.

CRUSTY OVERNIGHT NO-KNEAD BREAD

READY IN: 45 MINUTES PLUS 6–24 HOURS PROOFING MAKES: 1 LOAF

3½ cups plain flour, plus extra for dusting
1½ sachets instant yeast
1½ cups lukewarm water

This style of bread is a good option when you want a fresh loaf for weekend brunch or when friends are coming for dinner after work. Mix it together a day ahead; then all you need to do is raise and bake. No doughy hands or messy bench! You do need a heavy, heat-resistant casserole dish to bake it in.

1 Begin the bread at least 6 hours ahead of time. Combine all the ingredients in a bowl, stirring with a spoon until just combined; do not knead. Cover with oiled cling film and leave in a draught-free place for a minimum of 6 hours or preferably 12–24 hours.

2 Place a heatproof casserole dish (cast-iron, Pyrex, ceramic) in the centre of the oven with the lid on, and preheat the oven to its highest temperature. While the oven is heating, dust a piece of non-stick baking paper with flour and turn the dough out onto it. Do not knead – just shape as desired, tucking the edges under to smooth the top. Slash the top of the dough several times with a serrated knife, sprinkle with flour and let it rest until the oven is hot. Then, lift the dough on the paper and carefully place into the hot, ungreased casserole dish. Replace the lid.

3 Bake covered for 30 minutes, then remove the lid and bake for a further 15 minutes till browned and hollow-sounding when tapped on the bottom.

TIP: If the weather is very warm, proof the dough overnight in the fridge and bring it to room temperature before shaping and baking.

HUMMUS

READY IN: 10 MINUTES   MAKES: APPROX. 2 CUPS

HUMMUS

400g can chickpeas, rinsed and drained
½ cup tahini
2 cloves garlic, crushed
¼ cup lemon juice
½ tsp ground cumin
½ tsp salt
2 tbsp olive oil
a few tbsp iced water as needed

GARNISH – OPTIONAL

1 tbsp good olive oil
sprinkle of cumin or paprika
1 tsp lightly toasted cumin or pumpkin seeds

Serve this with bread (see photo on page 115), crackers or 'crudités' – which is simply another name for raw vegetables such as baby carrots, thin slivers of cucumber, radishes, cherry tomatoes, celery sticks, raw broccoli or cauliflower florets.

1 Place all the hummus ingredients in a food processor and pulse, adding iced water to achieve your desired consistency.

TIP: Hummus is a good base dip to which you can add other things. Try blending in roasted pumpkin or chargrilled capsicum, or a good dollop of natural yoghurt and a handful of chopped basil leaves.

MINTY PEA PESTO

READY IN: 10 MINUTES   MAKES: APPROX. 1¼ CUPS

2 cups frozen peas, boiled for 3 minutes then drained
2 cloves garlic, crushed
¼ cup mint leaves
2 tbsp extra virgin olive oil
2 tbsp blanched almonds or pine nuts
¼ cup grated Parmesan
squeeze of lemon juice
salt and pepper

I make this as a spread for crackers or bread (as pictured on page 115) when basil is out of season – I've pretty much always got peas in the freezer regardless of the time of year. You can make it more of a saucy consistency by splashing in some water. It's good as a quick sauce for pasta as well as a dip.

1 Process all the ingredients together, adding salt and pepper to taste. Add a dash of water if needed for a softer consistency.

SIMPLE SODA BREAD

READY IN: 50 MINUTES MAKES: 1 SMALL LOAF

- 1 cup milk
- 1 tbsp lemon juice or vinegar
- 2 cups plain flour, or 1 cup plain and 1 cup wholemeal, plus extra for dusting
- ½ tsp salt
- ½ tsp baking soda – sifted to remove lumps
- 1 tbsp sugar

Costing less than $2 a loaf and simple to make, soda bread was the saviour of many households during 2020's Covid-19 lockdown. It requires literally no breadmaking skill and no yeast, is ready in under an hour and makes a very tasty loaf. Best eaten the day it is made, it's great for short-notice picnics or pre-dinner drinks. Serve with Herbed Butter (see page 125), Hummus (page 113), Minty Pea Pesto (page 113) or a chunk of cheese. It also toasts well and is lovely with marmalade.

1 Preheat the oven to 200°C. Combine the milk and lemon juice or vinegar, and set aside for a few minutes to allow curdling to take place.

2 In a bowl or processor, combine the flour and salt, then add the sifted baking soda and the sugar. Mix or pulse with the curdled milk to form a wet dough.

3 Turn out on to a floured bench and, working quickly, knead lightly once or twice, then shape into a round loaf.

4 Press the loaf to flatten it, then transfer to a greased baking sheet. Dust the loaf with flour. Cut a deep cross in the top with a serrated knife, and bake for 35–40 minutes or until the loaf is well risen, nicely coloured and sounds hollow when tapped on the bottom.

TIPS: Have everything ready and the oven preheated, as the dough will begin to rise as soon as the milk and baking soda combine.

If you don't flatten the loaf it will take longer to cook, resulting in a very thick, hard crust.

REALLY GOOD CHEESE SCONES

READY IN: 25 MINUTES MAKES: 12

- 2 cups self-raising flour
- 2 cups grated tasty cheddar (a good one), plus extra for sprinkling
- pinch of salt
- approx. 1¼ cups milk

Another fan favourite, cheese scones are more than just something to bung in the lunchbox or picnic basket – they can elevate a soup (see page 66) or simple supper, turning it into a hearty real meal.

1 Preheat the oven to 200°C. In a bowl or processor, combine the flour, cheese, salt and any other seasoning ingredients you fancy, and pulse or mix until just combined. Pulse or mix in just enough milk to form a soft dough.

2 On a floured board, roll the dough out to a rectangle 3cm thick. Cut into 12 scones and arrange on a cold, greased baking tray. Sprinkle with extra cheese.

3 Bake for 10 minutes, or until well risen and crusty. Serve warm or cold.

TIP: Add other flavours to the dough, such as cooked onion and bacon, chopped sun-dried tomatoes, chorizo, roasted capsicum, feta or herbs. Or spread some chutney or pesto over the top before adding the sprinkle of cheese and baking.

SOFT FLOUR TORTILLAS

READY IN: AROUND 35 MINUTES   MAKES: 10–12 DEPENDING ON SIZE

2½ cups plain flour
1 tsp baking powder
1 tsp salt
3 tbsp oil
approx. ¾ cup warm water

Home-made flour tortillas are a world apart from bought ones. Soft and tender, they're amazing with scrambled eggs and salsa for brunch, as well as for burritos or soft tacos stuffed with pulled pork (see page 38).

1 Combine the dry ingredients in a bowl or processor, add the oil and then gradually add the warm water, pulsing or stirring just enough to form a dough.

2 Knead on a floured board till smooth and springy – about 5 minutes – then allow the dough to rest for a couple of minutes (this makes it easier to roll).

3 Divide the dough into 10–12 pieces, then roll out to circles roughly 18cm across. Cook the tortillas in a very hot, dry (no oil) frying pan for 30–60 seconds till they bubble and start to go brown. Turn them over and do the same on the other side. When cooked, wrap them in a damp tea towel to keep them soft.

4 To warm the tortillas, wrap them in foil and heat them in the oven, or leave them unwrapped, place them on a plate and microwave for 35 seconds.

TIP: If you have more than one rolling pin, rope in a family member to speed up the production, and heat two pans so you can cook them in half the time.

REALLY GOOD ROAST SPUDS

READY IN: APPROX. 50 MINUTES

- 1 medium-sized potato per person – more if feeding teenagers
- salt
- a decent slosh of oil
- 2 tbsp butter

The best roast potatoes are crispy, golden and sticky on the outside and fluffy on the inside. Choose a floury variety of potato, such as Agria.

1 Preheat the oven to 200°C. Peel the potatoes and cut into biggish pieces; too small and you will end up with all crispy crust and no fluffy spud.

2 Place in a large pot of cold water, add a pinch of salt and bring to the boil. Cook for 2-3 minutes, then drain. Return the pot of potatoes to the heat to dry out, shaking the pot to scuff and rough up the sides of the potatoes. Sprinkle lightly with salt.

3 Put the oil and butter in a large shallow roasting pan and heat in the oven. When the butter has melted, carefully tip in the potatoes and toss to coat in the hot fat.

4 Bake the spuds, turning occasionally, till crisp and golden. If you are cooking meat as well, the oven temperature will likely need to be lower. Put the spuds in anyway, then remove the meat when cooked, crank the temperature up high (220–230°) and give the spuds a blast for 15 or so minutes while the meat rests. The gentle cooking will have made them tender on the inside, and the hot finish will crisp them up.

TIP: You can roast any type of potato – they just produce different results.

SMASHED NEW POTATOES WITH GARLIC AND HERBS

READY IN: 50 MINUTES SERVES: 4

600g baby or new potatoes, scrubbed (or more as required)
3 tbsp olive oil
2 cloves garlic, minced
2 tbsp chopped herbs – basil, thyme or rosemary
salt and pepper

Cook these in the same pan as a pork meatloaf, as pictured on page 37, or other main dish. You can just crank up the temperature after the meat has cooked to make sure that the spuds are crisp.

1 Place the potatoes in a large pot of salted water. Bring to the boil, then cook, covered, for 15-20 minutes or until fork-tender. Drain thoroughly.

2 Preheat the oven to 190°C. Combine the oil, garlic and herbs.

3 Arrange the potatoes on a greased baking tray. Gently press the top of each one with a potato masher so that they are slightly flattened and cracked, then drizzle with the herby oil.

4 Place the tray in the middle of oven and roast for 40 minutes, or until golden and crispy. Increase the temperature for 10 minutes if needed. Season with salt and pepper.

CRISPY POTATO WEDGES

READY IN: 45 MINUTES SERVES: 4–6

- 4–6 floury or all-purpose potatoes, such as Agria
- 2 tbsp oil
- non-stick spray for the roasting pan, if you have it
- salt

A healthier alternative to chips, wedges are not only good as a side but, topped with salsa and grated cheese or chilli beans and sour cream, they also make a great filling snack for a crowd of hungry teens. You can season the wedges with spices, serve them with a dipping sauce, or just season them with salt as a weeknight side dish.

1 Preheat the oven to 230°C. Scrub the potatoes but leave the skin on. Cut in half longwise, then slice each half into three or four wedges.

2 Place the wedges in a bowl and add a tablespoon or two of oil. Rub the oil all over the wedges, then arrange in a single layer on a greased rimmed oven tray. Bake for 30–40 minutes, turning frequently, until crispy. Season with salt.

TIP: The skin of potatoes is often hailed as the most nutritious part. When peeling potatoes and kumara for a roast, I'll sometimes toss the peels in oil and bake to use as a snack or garnish.

MINTY SLAW

READY IN: 20 MINUTES SERVES: 6 AS A SIDE

3 cups green cabbage, shredded
⅓ cup mint, chopped
¼ cup parsley, chopped
1 large eating apple, skin on
⅓ cup mayonnaise
1 tbsp apple cider vinegar

1 Combine the cabbage, mint and parsley in a large bowl.

2 Grate half the apple and thinly slice the other half. Fold the grated apple into the cabbage mix.

3 Mix the mayonnaise and vinegar together, then mix through the salad. Fold in the sliced apple and chill till needed.

TIPS: Slaw is a great alternative to a leafy salad when lettuce and tomatoes are expensive.

Try the slaw as a filling in veggie burgers.

If you don't have fresh mint, you can use mint paste in the dressing.

DRESS IT UP

Different kinds of dressing suit different types of salad, so rather than make a big bottleful I just make what I need as I need it. Here are a few of my go-to recipes to try. They're all quick to make and will dress a normal-sized family salad.

POPPY SEED VINAIGRETTE

Good with a crunchy salad, or one that has a mix of vegetables and fruit.

⅛ cup white vinegar
1¼ tbsp white sugar
¼ tsp salt
¼ tsp mustard powder
½ tsp grated onion
¼ cup olive oil
1 tsp poppy seeds

1 Combine the ingredients in a screw-top jar and shake to mix.

LIME AND MAPLE DRESSING

This is good for tender mixed-leaf salads, as it won't weigh them down.

3 tbsp maple syrup
3 tbsp lime juice (approx. 2 limes)

1 Shake together in a screw-top jar and drizzle directly onto the salad.

BALSAMIC VINAIGRETTE

A bit more robust – great on a salad that is served alongside meat at a barbecue.

1 tbsp balsamic vinegar
4 tbsp extra virgin olive oil
½ clove garlic, crushed
½ tsp wholegrain mustard
pinch of sugar
salt and pepper

1 Combine the ingredients in a screw-top jar and shake to mix. Leave to stand for 10 minutes to allow the flavours to develop.

TIP: See also the Raspberry Basil Vinaigrette on page 106.

GARLIC BUTTER FOR GARLIC BREAD THE WAY YOU LIKE IT

READY IN: 10 MINUTES   MAKES: 100G, ENOUGH FOR 1 CRUSTY LONG LOAF

GARLIC BUTTER

100g butter, at room temperature
3 fat cloves garlic, crushed
handful of parsley, chopped

TO FINISH

1 baguette or crusty long loaf of French- or Italian-style bread

Use a basic supermarket baguette to add crispy, garlicky goodness and an instant upgrade to a modest meal.

1 Beat the butter in a small bowl till soft and creamy. Stir in the crushed garlic and chopped parsley.

2 For crunchy café-style garlic bread: Slice the bread into lengths and split longwise. Spread the cut sides generously with garlic butter, then refrigerate, with buttered sides together, till required. Grill cut side up, till golden and crispy.

3 For crispy-on-top, soft-inside, drippy-down-your-chin, pull-apart type garlic bread: Preheat the oven to 210°C. Cut the bread into thirds. Place each third on a sheet of foil. Slice diagonal slices at regular intervals along each piece of bread, and smear inside the slices generously with garlic butter. Wrap the foil over the top and bake for 15–20 minutes, then unwrap it enough to expose the bread and allow it to crisp slightly. Serve on a platter, straight from the foil.

TIP: Garlic varies in the intensity of its flavour. Smell the garlic butter before you use it. If you can't smell the garlic, use more.

HERBED BUTTER

READY IN: 5 MINUTES MAKES: APPROX. 100G

1 clove garlic, crushed
1 tbsp finely chopped fresh rosemary leaves
1 tbsp finely chopped chives
100g salted butter, at room temperature

This delicious butter will turn a humble chunk of bread into something special (see photo on page 115). It's also good for cooking fish, melting over vegetables, or adding flavour to pretty much anything. Butter freezes well, so you could make a double batch and tuck a couple of smaller logs in the freezer. You can then slice off a chunk to pop on top of a fish fillet, drop into potatoes as you mash them, or whip out to serve with bread when visitors are coming.

1 Blend the garlic and chopped herbs into the soft butter with the back of a spoon. Transfer to a sheet of non-stick baking paper, roll into a cylinder and twist the ends closed. Refrigerate and use as desired.

MARVELLOUS MEAT-FREE GRAVY

READY IN: 25 MINUTES MAKES: APPROX. 2 CUPS

⅓ cup dried mushrooms
2½–3 cups vegetable stock
1 tbsp olive oil
1 tbsp butter
1 large onion, chopped
3 cloves garlic, crushed
1 tsp dried thyme
1 sprig of rosemary
1 tbsp sherry
3 tbsp plain flour
2 tbsp soy sauce

This gravy is excellent with roast vegetables and, unlike a regular gravy, can be made as a sauce anytime you fancy it – whether you are cooking a roast or not.

1 Simmer the mushrooms gently in the stock for 5 minutes, then turn off the heat and leave to infuse. Melt the oil and butter in a saucepan, add the onion, garlic and herbs and cook gently till the onion is soft. Add the sherry, then stir in the flour.

2 Strain the stock, discarding the mushrooms. Gradually add the stock to the pan, whisking well after each addition. Stir continuously until thickened, then add the soy sauce. If you prefer a smooth gravy, pulse it in a blender or processor when done. Serve warm.

DESSERTS

So much in our society now seems to come with the promise of perfection, whether it's the 'perfect skin', 'perfect wedding' or the 'perfect pavlova'. In my experience, aiming for perfection is a needlessly stressful and generally disappointing aspiration, whatever the context. And since I'd much rather attend a really 'fun wedding' and scoff a 'delicious pavlova', I'm not going to promise you perfect desserts. I want to enjoy making something indulgent, not stress over it! With that in mind, I've included some recipes with 'mix and match' potential so you can add your own twist, or adapt to use ingredients you already have on hand – the goal being a delicious and memorable end to a meal.

BAKED BERRY SWIRL CHEESECAKE WITH ANY BERRY SAUCE

READY IN: 1 HOUR 10 MINUTES PLUS CHILLING SERVES: 8–10

A baked cheesecake is a bit of a treat, from a cost point of view, but goes a long way. They do tend to split, but I rather like the imperfections of home-made food and happily let the berry sauce fill any crevasses in my cheesecake.

ANY BERRY SAUCE

This sauce is also great with yoghurt, ice cream, porridge or pancakes.

- 200g (approx. 2 cups) berries – fresh or defrosted and drained; cut strawberries into pieces if using
- ¼ cup sugar
- 1 tbsp lemon juice, or to taste
- 2 tbsp water
- 1½ tsp arrowroot

CHEESECAKE

- 1½ packets of classic Oreo cookies (about 21)
- 45g butter, melted
- 500g cream cheese, at room temperature
- 2 tbsp plain flour
- 1 tsp vanilla essence
- 1 cup sour cream (a 250g tub)
- ¾ cup caster sugar
- 2 eggs, at room temperature

1 Make the sauce. Place the berries in a small saucepan with the sugar, lemon juice and water. Cover, bring to a simmer and cook until the berries are beginning to soften. Spoon out excess juice and, when cool, mix two tablespoons with the arrowroot, return it to the pan and heat gently, stirring until thick. Cool.

2 Preheat the oven to 150°C. Remove the base of a 22cm springform cake tin and turn it upside down (this makes it easier to remove the cake once chilled). Grease the tin and the inverted base, then cover the base with a piece of non-stick baking paper and clip it back into place, still upside-down, so that the excess paper is outside the tin. Place the tin on a rimmed baking tray.

3 Crush the biscuits in a sturdy bag with a rolling pin, or pulse in a processor. Mix in the melted butter, then spread evenly over the base, pressing down firmly. Chill in the fridge while you make the filling.

4 Beat the cream cheese with an electric beater until light and fluffy – around 1½ minutes. Add the flour, mixing until just combined. Add the vanilla, sour cream and sugar, mixing lightly. Mix in the eggs one at a time, then pour the mixture into the tin. Spoon a quarter of the cooled berry sauce on top and swirl it in with the tip of a knife. Bake for 45 minutes, or until light golden but still jiggly in the middle.

5 Turn off the heat and open the oven door slightly. Run a sharp knife around the cheesecake, separating it from the sides of the tin, then leave it in the oven till completely cool. Chill in the fridge before removing from the tin, to reduce splits forming. Serve in slices with extra berry sauce spooned over the top.

TIP: If you want to crack-proof your cheesecake, wrap the tin very well in foil and bake it in a water bath, then loosen the sides with a knife and chill it for 4 hours to allow the texture to firm up.

A BIG BOUFFY PAVLOVA WITH MAPLE CREAM

READY IN: 2 HOURS 10 MINUTES PLUS COOLING   SERVES: 8

6 egg whites
330g (1½ cups) caster sugar
1 tsp vanilla extract or essence
1 tsp white vinegar
2 tsp cornflour
2 cups cream
1½ tbsp icing sugar
3 tbsp maple syrup
prepared seasonal fruit
Any Berry Sauce (see page 128; optional)

Meringue is really inexpensive to make, so a show-stopper of a pav is a useful thing to have in your repertoire. Try a different flavoured cream (see page 137) and vary the toppings to suit the season, or use frozen berries made into a sauce when fresh are in short supply.

1 Preheat the oven to 175°C. Cover a rimless cookie sheet with non-stick baking paper.

2 Using a mixer or electric beater, beat the egg whites to soft peaks. Gradually beat in the caster sugar a spoonful at a time, until completely dissolved. Add the vanilla, then fold in the vinegar and cornflour.

3 Spoon the meringue onto the prepared tray to form a rectangle approximately 22cm x 32cm, using a spatula or palette knife to spread the meringue out. Try to avoid flattening it, as this will knock out the air. Aim for swirling, peaked mounds.

4 Reduce the oven temperature to 100°C and gently place the tray in the oven. Cook for 1 hour 30 minutes, then turn off the oven and leave in the oven until cooled completely. I often make it in the evening and leave it to cool in the oven overnight.

5 Slip a spatula under the pavlova to release it from the baking paper, and slide it gently onto a serving platter or tray.

6 Whip the cream to soft peaks. Fold in the icing sugar and maple syrup, and chill until needed. To assemble, top the meringue with cream and your fave fruit and sauce.

TIPS: For a bit of variation, swirl 1½ tablespoons cocoa into the meringue, or swirl in freeze-dried berry powder or pieces. You can add food colouring and flavouring if desired: try almond, or a hint of raspberry . . .

At Christmas you can use this recipe dolloped into a large wreath shape for a festive and pretty pud, or bake as individual big bouffy meringues to serve with cream or ice cream.

Store meringues in an airtight tin to keep them fresh.

CHOCOLATE NUTELLA TART

READY IN: 1 HOUR 45 MINUTES PLUS CHILLING SERVES: 10

PASTRY

230g (1½ cups) plain flour

75g toasted hazelnuts, skinned and pulsed to crumbs or hazelnut meal, plus a few extra, chopped, to garnish (optional)

¼ cup Dutch processed cocoa (darker than regular cocoa)

100g (⅔ cup) icing sugar

200g butter

2 egg yolks

FILLING

280g dark chocolate

1 cup cream

60g (3 tbsp) Nutella

GLAZE

½ cup cream

150g dark chocolate, chopped

1½ tbsp liquid glucose (see tips)

extra cream, to serve (optional)

This tart is always a hit. The delicate chocolate hazelnut pastry makes a little more than needed, so I cut the remainder into cookies (see the tips below), which when baked are really good sandwiched together with Nutella or jam. If you are in a rush, you can just make the tart with store-bought sweet shortcrust. You'll still get a great-tasting tart, but with a sweeter, golden-coloured crust.

1 Preheat the oven to 180°C. Make the pastry if using. Pulse the flour, hazelnut meal, cocoa, icing sugar and butter together to form crumbs. Add the egg yolks and pulse to mix. The mixture will look very dry, but gently squeeze and press it together. The heat from your hands will quickly form it into a dough.

2 Grease a 23cm loose-bottomed flan tin. Roll out the pastry and line the tin with an overhang of pastry all the way around. Trim off large excess bits, but retain an overhang. Line with non-stick baking paper and pastry weights. Bake for 20 minutes. Remove weights and paper, trim off excess and bake for a further 10 minutes. Cool.

3 Make the filling. Melt 30g (around 6 squares) of the chocolate and brush it over the base of the pastry. Chill in the fridge for 5 minutes, till set. Chop the remaining chocolate into small pieces.

4 Bring the cream to a simmer, remove from the heat and stir in the chopped chocolate. Stir till smooth, then stir in the Nutella and pour into the tin. Chill till set – around 1 hour.

5 Make the glaze. Combine the cream, chopped chocolate and glucose in a small saucepan. Heat gently, stirring, till melted. Pour over the tart and chill. Serve with cream and a scattering of chopped hazelnuts if desired.

TIPS: To use leftover chocolate hazelnut pastry, roll out to ½ cm thick, cut into bite-sized cookies and bake for 15 minutes.

The liquid glucose makes a shiny, glossy ganache, but if you don't have any you can omit it. Simply add the extra cream and chocolate to the filling. It won't be as shiny, but it will be just as delicious.

The tart also freezes well, unglazed, for 2–3 weeks, so can be made ahead, then defrosted and glazed on the day.

FUDGY CHOCOLATE PUDDING

READY IN: 45 MINUTES SERVES: 6–8

200g butter
300g (2 cups) brown sugar
1 tsp vanilla essence
4 eggs, lightly beaten
75g (⅔ cup) plain flour
50g (½ cup) cocoa
2 cups frozen cherries, defrosted (or other fruit)
100g dark chocolate, bits or chunks
⅓ cup hazelnuts, chopped or crushed
cream or ice cream, to serve

This dessert is best when just cooked and fudgy in the middle, as it tends to firm up a little on cooling. Add any fruit you like – I used frozen cherries, my personal fave, for the pudding in the picture, but canned peaches, pears or berries will all work well. It's the kind of dessert that's easy enough for a weeknight treat and good enough for guests.

1 Heat the oven to 190°C. Lightly grease a roughly 20cm x 30cm shallow ovenproof dish. Melt the butter in a saucepan, remove from the heat and stir in the sugar.

2 Add the vanilla, then mix in the eggs a bit at a time, beating well after each addition. Sift the flour and cocoa powder onto the mixture, and stir until thoroughly combined.

3 Pour into the prepared dish, and scatter with fruit, chocolate and nuts. Bake for 30 minutes, till crusty on the outside but still fudgy in the centre. Serve warm with cream or ice cream.

TIP: Place the hazelnuts in a sturdy bag and bash with a rolling pin to break them up.

GLUTEN-FREE DOUBLE-CRUST DESSERT PIE

READY IN: 1½ HOURS SERVES: 8

⅔ cup buckwheat flour
⅔ cup millet flour
⅔ cup tapioca flour
¼ cup brown rice flour, plus a little extra for rolling
1½ tsp xanthan or guar gum
½ tsp salt
4 tbsp sugar
½ tsp baking powder
½ tsp vanilla essence
pinch of ground cinnamon
230g cold butter, cubed
2 tsp apple cider vinegar
4–6 tbsp iced water
filling of choice

This pastry is flaky and light, with no nasty aftertaste or chalky texture. Despite the long ingredient list it's very easy to make and well worth the effort. Fill as you wish – the rhubarb and strawberry crumble filling on page 142 is a good one if you are struggling for ideas.

1 Place all the ingredients except the iced water in a food processor and pulse to form coarse crumbs. Pulse in enough iced water to make the mixture hold together when pressed.

2 Place onto a sheet of non-stick baking paper and divide into two slightly unequal portions. Flatten into thick discs and chill in the fridge for at least 30 minutes. While the pastry is chilling, prepare your chosen filling.

3 Roll the larger portion of dough between two sheets of non-stick baking paper to a size that fits the base of your pie dish, dusting lightly with brown rice flour to prevent sticking. Remove the top sheet of paper, then flip the pastry over onto the pan. Use the remaining paper to gently press the pastry into place, then peel it off. Use a slotted spoon to transfer the filling to the pie shell. Discard any excess juice.

4 Roll out the second portion of pastry in the same manner. Remove the top sheet of paper and cut some vents into the pastry before inverting it over the filling (if using decorative cutters for the vents, chill the pastry in the freezer for a few minutes to keep it from crumbling). Peel off the paper and crimp the edges of the pastry onto the rim of the pie dish. Bake for 30–40 minutes until biscuit-coloured.

TIP: Even people who aren't sensitive to gluten will happily eat this, so you don't have to make two separate desserts. I've also used it to make GF Christmas mince pies, jam tarts and other individual tartlets.

5 WAYS WITH WHIPPED CREAM

A flavoured whipped cream can transform a modest meringue or bowl of berries into a bona fide dessert. Try these cream variations for a lush next-level topping on anything from a store-bought sponge cake to a show-stopping trifle. They only take a few minutes to make!

COFFEE WHIPPED CREAM

2 tsp instant espresso powder, or 2½ tsp freeze-dried coffee granules
1 heaped tbsp sugar
1 cup cream

1 Stir the coffee and sugar into the cream. Whip as usual, tasting and adjusting the sweetness towards the end. Great with cherries and chocolate or on a pavlova.

GIANDUJA CREAM

1 cup cream
Nutella, at room temperature

1 Whip the cream to soft peaks, then fold in a big dollop of Nutella – adding more according to your taste. Serve with meringue, berries, or chocolate, banana or vanilla flavours, or use to fill profiteroles.

ORANGE BLOSSOM WHIPPED CREAM

1½ tsp sugar
1 tsp finely grated orange zest
orange flower water
1 cup cream

1 Stir the sugar, orange zest and a drop or two of orange flower water into the cream. Whip as usual, tasting and adjusting the flavour and sweetness as desired. Great with meringues, berries, sponge cake, fruit salad.

LEMON CURD CREAM

300ml cream
approx. ¼ cup lemon curd

1 Whip the cream to soft peaks, then swirl the curd through without mixing it in fully. Serve with meringue, pancakes, waffles, sponge cake or berries.

CHEAT'S CRÈME DIPLOMAT

1 cup cream
1 cup thick store-bought custard

1 Whip the cream to soft peaks, then fold the custard through. This quantity makes a good amount for a big pavlova or trifle. Some crushed praline folded in as well takes it to a whole other level. I also use crème diplomat for filling jam doughnuts.

SWEET PEACH AND RASPBERRY PIE

READY IN: 1½ HOURS PLUS CHILLING SERVES: 8

PASTRY

2½ cups plain flour
1 tbsp sugar
½ tsp salt
220g cold butter, cubed
¼ cup cold water
2 tsp white vinegar
1 egg white, to glaze
1 tbsp demerara sugar, to sprinkle (optional)

PEACH AND RASPBERRY FILLING

5 peaches, approx. 750g, peeled and sliced (or other fresh, canned, frozen or bottled fruit, such as cherries, plums, apricots or stewed apple)
¼–½ cup brown or white sugar
a squeeze of lemon juice
1 tbsp cornflour or arrowroot
1 cup raspberries (approx. 1 punnet – use more if you have them)

A good pie crust, along with whatever fruit you have on hand, can deliver a stunner of a dessert. This pastry will seem crumbly at first, but the warmth of your hands pressing the mixture together will soften the butter, laminating the pastry in layers, so the end result is a nicely textured pie crust.

1 Make the pastry. In a bowl or processor, combine the flour, sugar and salt. Pulse or cut in the butter until the pieces are pea-sized. Add the water and vinegar and mix lightly, then turn out onto the bench. The mixture will be crumbly. Don't knead; instead, use a lifting, folding and pressing motion to gather the crumbs, fold, press and repeat, until a dough forms – around 2 minutes. Roll into a log, divide into halves, flatten into discs, then wrap and chill 30 minutes.

2 Make the filling. Place the peaches, sugar and lemon juice in a saucepan and heat gently until the juices run. Pour juice into a bowl and when cooled, whisk in the cornflour or arrowroot, return to the pan and heat, stirring, until thickened. Cool completely.

3 Preheat the oven to 200°C. Dust a 23cm pie plate with flour. On a floured bench, roll out one pastry disc so it lines the dish with a 1½cm overhang. Place on a baking tray.

4 Pour in the filling and scatter with raspberries. Roll remaining pastry a little larger than the dish. Cut decorative shapes, if desired, for steam to vent. Lay pastry over the filling. Fold pastry overhang upwards onto the rim of the dish and crimp. Brush the pastry with the egg white, and sprinkle with the sugar if using.

5 Bake for 10 minutes, then reduce the temperature to 190°C and continue baking for a further 40 minutes, or until golden. If the edges are getting too brown, cover them (but not the rest of the pie) with foil. Serve warm or cold.

TIP: Canned or preserved fruit is likely to be sweeter than fresh, so taste the filling when you heat it and add only as much sugar as you need. Raw fruit may need some pre-cooking to begin the cooking process and release excess juice.

LOLLY CAKE JELLY TOP NO-BAKE CHEESECAKE

READY IN: 50 MINUTES PLUS CHILLING SERVES: 10

BERRY JELLY TOPPING

300g frozen raspberries, defrosted
1 tbsp cold water
1 tbsp sugar, or to your taste
1 tsp gelatine
1 tbsp boiling water

CHEESECAKE BASE

90g butter
¼ cup sweetened condensed milk
200g malt biscuits
125g 'Eskimo' lollies, roughly chopped
⅓ cup desiccated coconut (optional)

CHEESECAKE FILLING

1½ tsp powdered gelatine
2½ tbsp boiling water
250g cream cheese, at room temperature
⅓ cup caster sugar
1 tsp vanilla essence
150ml cream
2 tbsp desiccated coconut, to decorate (optional)

This pretty cheesecake is a playful trip down memory lane for anyone who grew up in New Zealand. The raspberry jelly topping is a little bit tart, balancing the sweetness of the base. The recipe could be used as a formula for a jelly-topped no-bake cheesecake with your own twist. See the tips below for suggestions.

1 Remove the base from a 20cm springform cake tin, turn the base upside down, cover with non-stick baking paper and clip into place. Line the inside of the tin with a strip of the paper and set aside.

2 Make berry purée. In a small saucepan, heat the raspberries, water and sugar until pulpy, then press through a sieve to remove seeds, and chill.

3 Make the base. In a small saucepan, gently heat butter and condensed milk till melted. Crush or process the biscuits to fine crumbs and place in a large bowl. Add milk mixture then, using your hands, work in the chopped lollies and coconut. Press mixture over base evenly and chill in the freezer while you make the filling.

4 Combine gelatine and water in a small bowl and set aside for 10 minutes. In a large bowl, beat cream cheese until soft and smooth. Add sugar, vanilla and cream and beat to soft peaks. Microwave the gelatine mixture for 15 seconds then, one at a time, stir 3 tablespoons of the cream mixture into the gelatine to 'temper' it.

5 Fold gelatine mixture into the cream cheese mixture, then pour into the prepared tin. Tap gently on the bench to level the top. Chill in the freezer until beginning to set, around 40 minutes.

6 Make the jelly. Whisk 1 teaspoon of gelatine into 1 tablespoon of boiling water. Stir into berry purée. Pour over cheesecake, then refrigerate until set. Gently release from tin and remove lining papers. Pat coconut around sides.

TIPS: Try a gingernut base: 250g gingernut biscuits and 90g melted butter.

You can make jelly from other puréed or sieved fruits for the top, or swirl (without gelatine) into the filling.

PROPER CRUMBLE WITH ROASTED RHUBARB AND STRAWBERRIES

READY IN: 50 MINUTES SERVES: 4–6

RHUBARB AND STRAWBERRY FILLING

400–450g rhubarb
150g (1 cup) fresh or frozen strawberries
2 tbsp brown sugar
3 tbsp orange juice
1 tsp cornflour or arrowroot (optional)

CRUMBLE TOPPING

120g cold butter, cubed
190g (1½ cups) plain flour
⅓ cup demerara sugar
pinch of cinnamon or mixed spice (optional)

Crumble is a great way to use up seasonal fruit. Mix and match any combination of stewed, canned or preserved fruits you have; you'll need at least 600g. Stewed or canned apple is a great base to which you can add other fruits, such as feijoa when in season.

This particular crumble topping is my favourite. The demerara sugar adds a 'mapley' flavour and a nice bit of scrunch. If you prefer, you can use regular white sugar or a mix of white and brown.

1 Preheat the oven to 190°C. Cut the rhubarb into 3cm pieces and place in an ovenproof dish. Scatter the strawberries, sugar and orange juice over the rhubarb. Bake for approx. 20 minutes, or until the rhubarb is cooked through but not falling apart. Meanwhile, make the crumble topping.

2 In a bowl or processor, combine the crumble ingredients and pulse or mash together to form lumpy, irregular crumbs.

3 Spoon a couple of tablespoons of juice out of the fruit in the dish, mix it with the cornflour or arrowroot and return it to the fruit. Stir in gently.

4 Sprinkle the crumble mix loosely over the cooked fruit. Return the dish to the oven and cook for 30–35 minutes, till the crumble is golden brown. Serve hot with custard or ice cream.

TIPS: Rhubarb is often sold in 400g bundles, but it's the easiest thing to grow.

The cornflour is simply to thicken the juices – if your fruit hasn't released much juice, you can leave it out.

Make a double batch of crumble topping and store in the freezer. Use it straight from the freezer to retain the chunky rustic texture.

Try different spices in the topping: ground ginger is great with feijoa crumble, and cinnamon, not surprisingly, works well with the classic apple.

Crumbles can be baked in individual dishes for single serves, which makes an everyday dessert seem a little bit more fancy.

SERIOUSLY GOOD 'SLAB PIE' WITH FLAKY CRISPY CRUST

READY IN: 1½ HOURS SERVES: 10

PASTRY

400g (3 cups + 3 tbsp) plain flour (not high grade)
300g cold butter, cubed
1½ tbsp brown sugar
250g cream cheese, cubed
1 tsp cider vinegar
2 tbsp iced water
beaten egg, to glaze
2 tbsp sugar, to sprinkle (optional)

PLUM FILLING

2 x 800g cans Black Doris plums, drained in a sieve and stones removed
¼–½ cup brown sugar
a squeeze of lemon juice
2 tbsp arrowroot

Sturdy enough for a picnic and elegant enough for dessert, this is the kind of pie that makes you fall in love with baking all over again. A processor is required for this pastry. It's a really good dessert for feeding a crowd, and it also freezes well, so can be made ahead. I use whatever fruit I have on hand, from home-bottled peaches to lightly cooked stewed apple, or just drained canned fruit without the juice. See the tips below for suggestions.

1 Make the pastry. Place the flour, butter, sugar and cream cheese in a processor and pulse to form a coarse crumb. Add the vinegar and iced water and pulse to mix. The dough will be crumbly at this point. Turn out onto the bench and press it, turning and folding, until it holds together. Cut into two uneven halves, flatten into thick discs with your palm, wrap and chill in the fridge for 30 minutes.

2 Preheat the oven to 200°C. Make the filling. Place the plums (or whatever fruit you are using) in a bowl with the sugar, lemon juice and arrowroot, and mix lightly.

3 Roll out the larger piece of dough so that it lines a slice tin approx. 23cm x 33cm with an overhang all the way around. Pour in the plums and liquid from the bowl.

4 Roll out the second piece of pastry to slightly larger than the dish, and cut it into wide ribbons. Lattice the dough ribbons over the top of the pie. Neaten the overhang with scissors, then fold the overhang inwards all the way around so that it rests on the rim of the tray. Crimp with your fingers.

5 Brush the pastry with beaten egg, sprinkle with sugar if desired, and bake for 35–45 minutes until deep golden.

TIPS: Some supermarket brands of cream cheese are only 225g, in which case you can make up the difference with extra butter.

Some suggestions for fillings: Try approx. 750g (around 5) peaches, peeled and sliced, and 1 cup of fresh or frozen berries or an equivalent quantity of other fruit. You can even use canned apple pie filling plus rhubarb or feijoa. If using a firm fruit like persimmons (very good with cranberries), I slice and microwave them for around 3 minutes first to soften them slightly.

STICKY BANANA PUDDING

READY IN: 1 HOUR SERVES: 8

- 1 cup pitted dates, coarsely chopped
- ¾ cup boiling water
- 1 tsp baking soda
- ½ tsp ground ginger
- 115g butter, at room temperature
- 1½ cups brown sugar
- 2 eggs
- 1 tsp vanilla essence
- 1 tsp baking powder
- pinch of salt
- 1½ cups plain flour
- 2 medium-sized bananas, mashed (around 1 cup; you can use frozen banana)
- 2 bananas, sliced longwise, to decorate (optional)

TOFFEE RUM SAUCE – OPTIONAL

- 100g butter
- 1 packed cup brown sugar
- 2 tbsp rum or spiced rum (optional)
- ½ cup cream

Great as a family dessert with custard or cream, and good enough for guests with the addition of the Toffee Rum Sauce. If you really want to make an impact, bake it in individual well-greased cups or ramekins and turn them out onto plates before serving (reduce the cooking time accordingly; see the tips below). This pud freezes well, too.

1 Preheat the oven to 180°C. Grease a medium-sized baking dish. Place the dates in a heatproof bowl, cover with the boiling water and stir in the baking soda and ginger.

2 Cream the butter and sugar in a bowl or processor. Beat in the eggs one at a time, then the vanilla.

3 Add the baking powder and salt to the flour, then add half the flour to the butter mixture, stir briefly, then add half the dates and stir briefly again. Repeat with the remaining flour and dates, then mix until all is just combined. Fold in the mashed banana and pour into the prepared dish. Arrange the sliced bananas on top if using.

4 Bake for 50–60 minutes, or until the pudding is springy and a knife inserted into it comes out clean.

5 While the pudding is cooking, make the sauce. In a saucepan, melt the butter and sugar together and heat until bubbling. Cook for 2 minutes, add the rum and stir, add the cream and stir, then simmer for 5 minutes or till thickened. The sauce will harden on cooling, so reheat it before serving.

TIPS: The dates add sweetness and a lovely dark colour to the dish; they don't make it taste like dates, so date-haters can relax.

You could omit the rum from the sauce, or switch it out for Baileys or whisky if you prefer. I sometimes buy a 'miniature' of a spirit I want to use in cooking, as it's more affordable.

There is no hard and fast rule for adjusting cooking times due to the variations between vessels such as tea or coffee cups, ramekins, dariole moulds, mini loaf pans or muffin tins. I start by reducing the cooking time by two thirds, and then check at 5-minute intervals till risen and springy. Make a note of the cooking time beside the recipe for next time.

LIME PANNA COTTA WITH RUM SYRUP

READY IN: 20 MINUTES PLUS 4 HOURS CHILLING   SERVES: 6

LIME PANNA COTTA

non-stick cooking spray to grease moulds
500ml cream
200ml milk
¾ cup caster sugar
1 tsp finely grated lime zest
¼ cup lime juice
2 tsp powdered gelatine

RUM SYRUP

¼ cup maple syrup
⅛ cup brown sugar
1–2 tbsp dark rum (optional)

Panna cotta is a bit of a posh pud that's secretly cheap and easy to make. You can set it in pretty glasses, or use moulds and turn them out to serve. I've made so many versions in recent years, but this is a good basic one to kick you off.

1 Grease six pudding cups approx. 120ml capacity, or glasses or tea cups, with non-stick cooking spray.

2 Place the cream, milk, sugar and lime zest in a saucepan over medium heat. Cook, stirring, for 5–7 minutes until almost simmering. Remove from the heat. Add the lime juice and gelatine, and stir well to combine. Set aside for 10 minutes for the flavours to develop.

3 Strain the mixture through a fine sieve into a large jug. Discard the lime zest. Stir gently, then pour the mixture into the prepared dishes. Refrigerate for 4 hours or overnight.

4 Make the syrup. Combine the ingredients in a small saucepan and bring to a simmer over medium heat. Simmer for 2 minutes until slightly thickened. Set aside to cool before using.

5 Either serve in the dishes or turn out: run a small knife around the edge of the moulds. Dip the base of each mould very briefly in hot water. Invert over a dessert plate and give a single good hard shake. The panna cotta should plop onto the plate. Add a spoonful of cooled syrup when serving, if desired.

TIPS: Make sure that the gelatine is fully dissolved to ensure a silky, even set.

Mix and match flavours – try vanilla, lemon, gin, chai, coffee . . . infusing the liquid with your chosen flavour. Once you have mastered the basic technique, you can play around. For example, switching some of the cream for yoghurt creates a fresher, more tangy result.

Once set, panna cotta are quite stable, so can be transported if you are taking a dessert to someone else's place.

If drizzling with a sauce, a cold one is better, as warm sauce will melt the delicate custard.

CAKES AND OTHER BAKING

Home baking isn't just good for the budget, it's also good for the brain. When we bake, we engage in a sensory-focused activity that occupies the whole mind-body spectrum. Because it requires concentration, the mind is prevented from ruminating. It's like a kind of 'mindfulness', with an awesome edible result that produces feelings of wellbeing for both the baker and their grateful household. It's recognised as a legitimate form of behavioural activation, with well-researched therapeutic benefits including improved mood and reduced anxiety.

Baking also allows us to express ourselves when words simply won't cut it. Whether it's a cake for a grieving friend, lunchbox baking for the family with the new babe, or the batch of handcrafted cookies you give as a thank you, there is so much more to be gained from a batch of baking than saving a few cents at the supermarket.

APRICOT, CRANBERRY AND MIXED SEED MUESLI BARS

READY IN: 35 MINUTES MAKES: 12–16

1½ cups rolled oats
¼ cup maple syrup
¼ cup honey
3 tbsp peanut butter (or your preferred nut butter)
1 tsp vanilla essence
½ cup mixed seeds – pumpkin, sesame, sunflower . . .
1 tbsp chia seeds
⅓ cup desiccated coconut
¼ cup dried cranberries, chopped
¼ cup dried apricots, chopped

These scrummy bars more than make up for their slight crumbliness with a lovely nutty texture, loads of flavour and substantially less refined sugar and fat than regular bars. Plus they're dairy-free, wheat-free and (depending on your relationship with oats) also gluten-free. You can make this recipe vegan by swapping the honey for agave syrup or another vegan honey alternative.

1 Preheat the oven to 180°C. Line a 27cm x 17cm (approx.) baking tin or dish with non-stick baking paper.

2 Place the oats on a baking tray and toast in the oven for 15 minutes, or until lightly golden. While the oats are toasting, combine the syrup, honey and peanut butter and heat in a saucepan or microwave until liquid. Add the vanilla and mix together.

3 Place the toasted oats, all the seeds, and the coconut, cranberries and apricots in a bowl. Add the warm liquid and mix. Tip into the prepared tin and press firmly into place with a wet hand, then cover with baking paper and roll over with a can from your pantry to neaten.

4 Bake for 10–15 minutes, till lightly golden. Cool in the tin for 5 minutes; then, while still warm, score into bars with a knife but do not cut completely through. When completely cool, lift from the tin and slice into bars.

TIPS: I've made these with different combinations of seeds and dried fruit (I particularly like dried mango).

If you fancy adding chocolate, around ¼ cup of chocolate chips is sufficient. Let the raw mixture cool a little before adding them, or they might melt before they get near the oven.

BANANA SHEET CAKE WITH PEANUT BUTTER BUTTERCREAM

READY IN: 45 MINUTES
MAKES: 1 SHEET CAKE, OR ONE 20CM ROUND CAKE, OR TWO 20CM SANDWICH CAKES

110g butter
175g (¾ cup) sugar
2 eggs
2 medium-sized ripe bananas, mashed
1 tsp baking soda
2 tbsp boiling milk
225g (1¾ cups) self-raising flour
½ tsp baking powder

PEANUT BUTTER BUTTERCREAM

110g butter, at room temperature
½ cup peanut butter – we like a chunky one, but use what you prefer
3 cups icing sugar
¼ cup milk
¼ cup roasted peanuts, chopped, to decorate

CHOCOLATE DRIZZLE - OPTIONAL

75g dark chocolate, broken into pieces
1 tsp oil

Sheet cakes are simply cakes baked in a large, shallow tin. The advantage is that you get more serves from the same recipe. I sling the whole thing together in the food processor, which makes it very quick and easy. If you don't fancy the Peanut Butter Buttercream, see the tips below for other topping suggestions.

1 Preheat the oven to 180°C. Grease and line the base of a Swiss roll tin approx. 23cm x 33cm, or a 20cm loose-bottomed tin or two 20cm loose-bottomed sandwich tins.

2 In a bowl or processer, beat the butter and sugar until pale and creamy, then add the eggs and beat well. Mix in the mashed banana.

3 Combine the baking soda and boiling milk and stir into the mixture. Mix in the flour and baking powder and pour into the prepared tin or tins. Level the top, then bake for 25–30 minutes, or until risen, golden and springy. For sandwich tins, bake for around 20 minutes till risen and springy. Turn out onto a rack to cool.

4 Make the buttercream. Use electric beaters to beat the butter and peanut butter together until pale. Add 1 cup of icing sugar and beat until light, and repeat with a second cup of icing sugar. Add half the milk and mix, then add the remaining cup of icing sugar, along with just enough milk to make a light, airy consistency. Spread over the cooled cake with a spatula or palette knife.

5 If using the chocolate, melt it in a bowl set over a pan of simmering water (but not touching the water). Stir in the oil, then drizzle over the top of the buttercream. Sprinkle with chopped peanuts.

TIPS: The banana cake can be simply dusted with icing sugar, or try the chocolate frosting from Dana's Chocolate Cake (page 174), or for something a bit more special try the Milk Chocolate Mousse Frosting on page 170.

Ripe bananas are often cheaper to buy and can be frozen. They're very mushy when defrosted, making them super easy to mash or mix for using in baking.

This is an easy recipe to double: 'one for now and one for the freezer'. I've even tripled it and baked it in a roasting pan. It was a lot of cake, but since it freezes well there's never any waste.

BLUEBERRY SHORTCAKES WITH LEMON DRIZZLE

READY IN: 35 MINUTES   MAKES: 12

- 90g butter
- 2 cups self-raising flour
- ½ tsp baking powder
- ¼ cup brown sugar
- 1 tsp lemon zest
- ¼ tsp vanilla essence
- 1 cup cream, or ½ and ½ milk and yoghurt or milk and sour cream
- 1 cup blueberries, fresh or frozen
- 1 tbsp sugar

LEMON DRIZZLE

- a good squeeze of lemon juice
- ⅓ cup icing sugar
- a drop of water or milk
- ¼ cup toasted flaked almonds, to decorate (optional)

From the same family as scones, these little treats are quick to make and don't need any jam or cream, so are good for a lunch box or picnic basket. You can mix and match with different fruits and flavours – cherry with almond essence is good, as is raspberry and white chocolate.

1 Preheat the oven to 200°C. Chill the butter in the freezer for 10 minutes. Place the flour, baking powder, brown sugar and lemon zest in a bowl and mix. Grate in the chilled butter and mix gently with a knife.

2 In a measuring jug, add the vanilla to the cream and pour into the flour mix. Reserve the cream jug with its creamy residue. Mix the ingredients in the bowl with a knife, then turn out on to a lightly floured bench and knead gently around 10 times, turning over once or twice until the dough just holds together.

3 Roll or pat the dough into a rectangle. With a short side nearest you, fold the dough into thirds (like you would fold a towel), pulling the bottom third up over the centre and then folding the top third over that. Turn the dough so that the folded edge faces you, roll or pat into a rectangle again, and fold again. Turn the dough so that the folded side faces you and repeat one more time.

4 Dust the bench lightly with flour and roll the dough into a rectangle approx. 34cm long x 23cm wide. With the long side facing you, scatter the blueberries over the lower two-thirds of the rectangle. Fold the top third over to cover half the berries, then lift and fold it over again to cover the bottom third, making a long strip with the berries layered in it. Neaten the ends.

5 Add a splash of water to the cream residue in the jug and brush this over the rectangle. Sprinkle with the sugar. Divide the strip into 6 squares, then cut each diagonally to make 12 triangles. Place on a greased baking tray and bake for 15 minutes, or until risen and lightly browned. Cool on a wire rack.

6 When cooled, combine the lemon juice and icing sugar with just enough water or milk to allow it to drizzle off the end of a knife. Drizzle the glaze over the shortcakes, then scatter on the flaked almonds if using.

BUTTERMILK CHOC CHIP SCONES

READY IN: 35 MINUTES MAKES: 12 OR MORE

- 3 cups plain flour
- 3 tsp baking powder
- 2 tbsp sugar
- 60g butter, chopped
- 1¼ cups buttermilk, either store-bought or home-made (combine 1¼ tbsp lemon juice with 1¼ cups milk, and leave for 5 minutes or until curds form)
- ⅓ cup chocolate chips

Acidulated dairy products like buttermilk, sour cream and yoghurt give baked goods a very tender crumb. Even when making regular scones I'll sour the milk with a squeeze of lemon, but using buttermilk results in a lovely fluffy scone. And the chocolate chips – well, when didn't chocolate make everything better? You can leave them out if you prefer a plain scone.

1 Preheat the oven to 200°C. Grease and flour a square cake tin or a flat cookie sheet.

2 Place the flour, baking powder, sugar and butter in a processor or large bowl. Pulse, or use your fingertips to rub the butter into the flour, until the mixture resembles fine breadcrumbs.

3 Add the buttermilk and chocolate chips, and pulse or stir until the dough comes together. Place on a lightly floured surface.

4 Roll out to a rectangle 3cm thick. Cut into 12 scones, or more if you want them smaller. Place in the prepared tin or tray. Bake for 15–17 minutes, or until light golden and hollow-sounding when tapped on top.

TIPS: Handle scone dough as little as possible. Scones should be light and fluffy; kneading or working the dough activates the gluten in the flour and makes a strong, elastic dough that's great for bread but not for scones.

If you want round scones, cut the dough with a cookie cutter, re-rolling and cutting the trimmings.

QUICK LOW-SUGAR CHIA JAM

READY IN: 15 MINUTES PLUS COOLING MAKES: 1 CUP

2 cups berries, fresh or frozen
2 tbsp maple syrup
2 tbsp chia seeds
½ tsp vanilla essence

This is great for using up odds and ends of frozen berries, or for those who are never going to get into serious jam-making but want something special to spread on their toast, scones or sammies.

1 Combine the fruit and syrup in a saucepan and simmer gently until pulpy. Add the chia seeds and vanilla and mix well. Leave to thicken. Cover and store in the fridge for up to 2 weeks.

TIP: If you don't have 2 cups of berries, make up the difference with other fruit such as apple or pear that has been grated or chopped small. Simmer over a low heat with the berries for 10 minutes or until pulpy. Mash any fruit chunks to an even consistency.

EASY LEMONY BERRY DANISH

READY IN: 50 MINUTES PLUS DEFROSTING SERVES: 8

- 400g block of flaky puff pastry, defrosted
- 1–2 tbsp plain flour, for rolling the pastry
- 100g cream cheese
- ¼ cup lemon curd
- 1 tsp vanilla essence
- ¾ cup frozen or fresh raspberries or blueberries
- 1 egg, lightly beaten

VANILLA GLAZE

- ¾ cup icing sugar, plus extra to dust
- 1 tsp vanilla essence
- 2 tbsp milk

It's a bit of a cheat to call this a Danish, because it doesn't use a yeast-raised dough, but it does taste like something from a real bakery and is great for a morning tea or an easy dessert. Block pastry takes several hours to defrost, so you'll need to plan this one ahead.

1 Preheat the oven to 200°C. Dust the bench lightly with flour, and roll the pastry out to a rectangle approx. 27cm x 33cm, dusting with flour as needed. Divide the pastry longwise into slightly unequal halves. Transfer the narrower half to a greased baking sheet.

2 In a small bowl, beat the cream cheese with a knife till softened and smooth, then mix in the lemon curd and vanilla. Spread the mixture down the centre of the pastry strip on the baking sheet, leaving a 1cm border either side.

3 Scatter on the berries and brush the borders with water. Lay the remaining pastry over the top, pressing the edges firmly to seal. Brush generously with the beaten egg and slice 8–10 vents in the top of the pastry to release steam.

4 Bake for 25 minutes, or until golden and risen. Combine the glaze ingredients and drizzle over the top. Dust with extra icing sugar before serving.

TIP: Serve the Danish with cream or ice cream as an easy dessert.

CHOCOLATE CHIP COOKIES

READY IN: 40 MINUTES MAKES: 50+ DEPENDING ON SIZE

1 tsp baking soda
1 tsp salt
3¼ cups plain flour
250g butter, at room temperature
1 cup brown sugar
1 cup white sugar
2 eggs
2 tbsp hot water
2 tsp vanilla essence
1–2 cups chocolate chips, morsels or chunks

This recipe is a much-loved fan favourite. It makes a lot – brilliant for when you want a treat to send off to camp with the kids or to take away on holiday. The dough can also be rolled and frozen unbaked; bake from frozen as needed. Or bake the whole lot and freeze half; just make sure you hide them under the frozen peas, where the kids will never look.

1 Preheat the oven to 180°C. Lightly grease two rimless cookie sheets and set aside. Sift the baking soda and salt into the flour and set aside.

2 In a bowl or processor, combine the butter and both sugars and beat until pale and creamy. Add the eggs, hot water and vanilla and mix, then mix in the flour to make a stiff dough. Fold in the chocolate chips.

3 Scoop teaspoonfuls of mixture, roll lightly into balls and place on the greased trays, allowing room for spreading. Bake for 8–10 minutes, or until golden brown, rotating the trays if needed. Transfer to cooling racks. The cookies will firm up on cooling.

TIPS: You can use a mix of white and dark chocolate, or chocolate chips and nuts. The cookies can be warmed in the microwave for a minute to soften, then sandwiched together with ice cream for an easy dessert.

If making in a food processor, make sure you mix the chocolate chips in by hand so they don't get chopped to smithereens.

BAKED WITH LOVE
HOME MADE
EAT ME

GINGERBREAD BISCUITS

READY IN: 1 HOUR   MAKES: AROUND 30 DEPENDING ON SIZE

- 125g butter, at room temperature
- ½ cup golden syrup
- ½ cup firmly packed brown sugar
- 1 egg yolk
- 2½ cups plain flour, sifted
- 1 tbsp ground ginger
- 1 tsp ground cinnamon
- ¼ tsp ground cloves

This is my current favourite gingerbread recipe. It's easy, with a good amount of spice, holds together for fiddly stuff like cutting out gingerbread people and retains a nice sharp imprint if I'm stamping the cookies with a stamp (see photo on previous page).

1 In a medium-sized bowl, beat the butter, syrup and sugar with an electric mixer until creamy and paler in colour. Add the egg yolk and beat until just combined. Add the sifted flour and spices and stir until the mixture forms a dough.

2 Knead the dough gently on a lightly floured bench until smooth, then wrap and chill in the fridge for half an hour.

3 Preheat the oven to 180°C. Grease two oven trays. Roll the dough out on a lightly floured bench to approx. 3mm thick. If using cookie stamps, dip them in flour and tap off any excess. Stamp the dough, then place cutters around the stamped portion to cut out. You don't have to use cookie cutters – you can cut them out with the rim of a glass or simply cut into rectangles with a knife.

4 Arrange on trays, about 3cm apart. Bake for 10 minutes, or until light golden. Let them sit on the trays for 5 minutes before transferring to wire racks to cool.

TIPS: Store in an airtight container, or freeze either cooked or uncooked.

You can use any clean stamp for stamping the dough; I use wooden fabric stamps as well as proper cookie stamps. I have gathered a lot of cookie cutters over the years from charity shops – I pretty much never buy them new.

OATY CHOCOLATE CHUNK COOKIES

READY IN: 40 MINUTES MAKES: 30–36

- 225g butter, at room temperature
- 1 cup brown sugar
- 1 tbsp golden syrup
- 1½ cups plain flour
- 1½ cups rolled oats
- 1 tsp baking powder
- a dash of milk (roughly ⅓ cup, or as needed)
- 1 cup (or more) chocolate morsels, chips or chunks

These scrummy oat and chocolate bikkies (see photo on page 165) are just the thing to have with a cold glass of milk. For extra indulgence, ping the cookies in the microwave for a few seconds before eating, to make the choccy chunks soft and gloriously gooey.

1 Preheat the oven to 180°C. Grease two baking trays.

2 In a bowl or processor, cream the butter and sugar until pale and fluffy. Mix in the golden syrup, then stir in the flour, oats, baking powder and milk, adding just enough milk to form a stiff but rollable dough.

3 Lastly, stir in the chocolate chips. Roll the mixture into balls, or just blob onto the prepared trays, with a 3cm gap between them.

4 Bake for 15 minutes, or until lightly browned. Cool on racks.

TIPS: You can use white chocolate chunks, if you prefer, or a mix.

If using a processor, be sure to stir the chocolate and oats in by hand, or the processor may chop them to shreds.

STICKY APRICOT AND KUMARA SPICE CAKE

READY IN: 1 HOUR 30 MINUTES PLUS COOLING   SERVES: 10

½ cup canned apricots
⅓ cup apricot jam
around 250g kumara, peeled
4 eggs
200g (1¼ cups) brown sugar
1 cup canola oil
3 cups self-raising flour
½ tsp baking soda
2 tsp ground ginger
3 tsp ground cinnamon
1 tsp ground nutmeg
½ tsp ground cardamom
¾ cup natural unsweetened yoghurt

TOPPING

⅓ cup apricot jam
½ cup flaked almonds
icing sugar, for dusting (optional)

Root vegetables are naturally sweet and add interesting texture and subtle sweetness to baked goods for little cost. Kumara, carrot, pumpkin, beetroot and parsnip are all viable candidates, and oil is cheaper than butter, so a big cake like this doesn't have to cost a lot. Be sure to use a large cake tin, though.

In the spirit of full disclosure, it was hectic preparing all the dishes to be photographed for this book, and in my haste I baked the one pictured in the wrong tin, which was too small, meaning that it was still raw in the middle after an hour in the oven. Use the right tin and yours will be a bit larger and not quite as high, and it will also be properly cooked all the way through!

1 Preheat the oven to 180°C. Grease and line the base and sides of a 22–23cm cake tin. Mash the apricots and jam together and set aside. Grate the kumara and set aside.

2 In a large bowl, beat the eggs and sugar until thickened and pale – a milky coffee colour. With the beater running, trickle in the oil. Fold in the grated kumara, then add the dry ingredients and spices. Lastly, fold in the yoghurt.

3 Pour half the batter into the prepared cake tin, scatter the apricot and jam mixture over, then cover with the remaining cake batter.

4 Bake for 50–60 minutes, or till a skewer inserted into the middle comes out clean. Cool on a wire rack.

5 Make the topping. Stir the apricot jam till smooth. Spread over the top of the cooled cake, and sprinkle the almonds over the jam. Dust the cake with icing sugar if using. Serve in slices with whipped cream, or warm in the microwave and serve for dessert with custard or cream.

TIP: I like the simple apricot jam glaze, but you could use cream cheese icing if you want it to be fancy.

FUDGY CHOCOLATE CAKE WITH MILK CHOCOLATE MOUSSE FROSTING

READY IN: 1 HOUR PLUS COOLING SERVES: 10 AS A LAYER CAKE OR 16 AS A SHEET CAKE

- 225g dark chocolate (I use 62% cocoa), broken into squares
- 60ml vegetable oil (such as soybean or canola)
- 2 eggs
- 1 cup brown sugar
- ¾ cup plain flour
- ½ tsp baking soda
- ½ tsp baking powder
- ¼ cup cocoa, sifted
- ¼ tsp salt
- 2 tsp vanilla essence
- ⅓ cup maple syrup
- 1 cup ground almonds
- ¼ cup milk
- 1 large raw beetroot (approx.) peeled, grated and squeezed of excess liquid, to give 250g

MILK CHOCOLATE MOUSSE FROSTING

- 220g milk chocolate, broken into squares
- 220g butter, at room temperature
- 1½ cups icing sugar
- 1 tbsp golden syrup
- edible flower petals, to decorate (optional)

Not your everyday chocolate cake – and, I'll be honest, not exactly cheap to make; this is a special-occasion cake. Delicate, with a subtle sweetness, it's the ideal carrier for my Milk Chocolate Mousse Frosting, or chocolate ganache, or a salted caramel buttercream. I've also baked this mixture as a sheet cake in a 23cm x 33cm Swiss roll tin.

1 Preheat the oven to 180°C. Grease and line the bases of two 20cm loose-bottomed cake tins.

2 In a heatproof bowl set over a saucepan of simmering water (not touching it), combine the dark chocolate and oil and heat until melted. Set aside to cool.

3 In a bowl or processor, beat the eggs and sugar till lightened in colour. Sift in the flour, soda, baking powder, cocoa and salt. Add the vanilla, maple syrup, ground almonds and melted chocolate, pulse or mix together, then mix in the milk. Lastly, fold in the grated beetroot.

4 Pour into the prepared tins and bake for 30–40 minutes, or until a skewer inserted into the middle comes out clean. When cool enough to handle, gently remove from the tins and cool completely on a rack.

5 Make the frosting. Melt the milk chocolate in a heatproof bowl set over a pan of simmering water (not touching it), then remove from the heat to cool. When cool, beat the butter and sugar with an electric mixer till pale – at least 3 minutes. Beat in the golden syrup, then beat in the cooled melted chocolate. Spread half the mixture over each cake and stack one on top of the other. Decorate as desired.

TIPS: I wear rubber gloves when peeling beetroot, and I dump the grated beet into an old tea towel to wring out the excess moisture.

In hot weather, buttercream frostings can split or curdle. To repair a split buttercream, place the bowl in a bowl of iced water and beat it again.

FUDGE CAKE SLICE

READY IN: 30 MINUTES PLUS CHILLING MAKES: 24 SERVES, DEPENDING ON SIZE

- 1 packet of plain biscuits – wines, malts, whatever is cheap
- 1½ cups desiccated coconut
- 1 cup raisins, sultanas or Craisins
- 395g can sweetened condensed milk
- 2 tbsp cocoa
- 150g butter
- 1 tsp vanilla essence

ICING

- 1½ cups icing sugar
- 3 tbsp cocoa
- 3 tbsp butter, at room temperature
- 2 tbsp hot water
- ½ tsp vanilla essence
- 100s and 1000s, to decorate (optional)

This recipe has been a fan favourite for over a decade. Cut it into slices for the kids or into tiny squares as a treat with your cuppa. It also freezes well, so you can stash a few squares away for when no one is looking.

1 Grease and line a Swiss roll tin or slice tray. Crush the biscuits in a sturdy bag or pulse in a processor, then combine with the coconut and raisins in a large bowl.

2 Place the condensed milk, cocoa and butter in a small saucepan. Heat till bubbling, stirring frequently to prevent scorching. Remove from the heat and add the vanilla.

3 Stir the hot mixture into the dry ingredients till thoroughly combined. Press into the greased tin, then refrigerate or slip into the freezer till cooled and firm.

4 Make the icing. Combine the icing ingredients in a bowl or processor and spread over the cooled slice using a spatula or palette knife. Sprinkle with 100s and 1000s if using. Chill to set the icing before slicing into bars.

TIP: If coconut allergy is a problem, substitute rolled oats; my sister always made this with oats, as her kids simply didn't like coconut.

DANA'S CHOCOLATE CAKE

READY IN: 1½ HOURS PLUS COOLING MAKES: 1 DEEP 20CM CAKE, SERVING 12; OR 16 REGULAR CUPCAKES; OR 12 REGULAR AND 24 MINI CUPCAKES; OR AROUND 60 MINIS

If making as cupcakes, you'll need more frosting – about 1½ times the quantity usually made for a single cake. This is also a great frosting for banana cake or no-bake slices such as Fudge Cake Slice (page 172).

1⅔ cups plain flour
1½ cups sugar
⅔ cup cocoa
1½ tsp baking soda – yes, baking soda! (see tips)
1 tsp salt
1½ cups milk
100g butter, melted
2 eggs

FROSTING
250g icing sugar
100g butter, melted
⅓ cup cocoa, sifted
1 tsp vanilla essence
a splash of milk to mix

FILLING – OPTIONAL
¼ cup jam

Arguably the most frequently made chocolate cake in the country! The Dana's Chocolate Cake page is invariably the most splattered and tattered page in people's old *destitute gourmet* cookbooks, and for good reason. It's easy to make, uses stuff you already have in the pantry, carves well for shaped birthday cakes, and can be made dairy-free, gluten-free or egg-free – or even all three – with little noticeable difference. Expect it to rise a lot and probably crack a bit on top – despite this it always looks and tastes great.

1 Preheat the oven to 180°C. Grease and line the base and sides of a 20cm loose-bottomed cake tin.

2 In a bowl or processor, combine all the cake ingredients and pulse or beat with a mixer, scraping down the sides once or twice till evenly blended. Pour the mixture into the prepared tin.

3 Bake for 1 hour 10 minutes or until risen, springy and a skewer inserted into the middle comes out clean. Cool in the tin for a few minutes, then cool completely on a rack.

4 Make the frosting. Place the icing sugar, melted butter and cocoa in a processor, pulse to combine, then add the vanilla and mix, adding just enough milk to give a spreadable consistency.

5 To assemble, slice the cake in half horizontally. Spread jam, if using, on the cut side of the bottom half, then spread frosting on the cut side of the top half. Sandwich together. Pile the remaining frosting on top, and use a spatula or palette knife to work it over the top and down the sides, coating the cake. Place in the fridge to firm the frosting, if desired.

TIP: Baking soda is pure sodium bicarbonate. When combined with moisture and an acidic ingredient (e.g. yoghurt, chocolate, cocoa, buttermilk, honey), a chemical reaction is immediately triggered that produces bubbles of carbon dioxide that expand and lift the mixture. This type of raising agent needs to be baked immediately after mixing, so have the tins or cupcake pans ready and the oven hot before you mix. Baking powder contains baking soda but not in sufficient quantity for this mixture (in case you were planning to email to check).

LEMONY CUSTARD SLICE

READY IN: 35 MINUTES PLUS SEVERAL HOURS CHILLING SERVES: 12-16

- 2 sheets frozen puff pastry, defrosted
- ½ cup custard powder
- ½ cup caster sugar
- 1 tbsp lemon zest (1-2 large lemons)
- 2½ cups milk
- 2 cups cream
- 1 egg yolk
- ½ tsp vanilla essence
- ⅓ cup lemon juice (1-2 large lemons)

GLAZE

- 1 tsp butter, at room temperature
- 1¼ cups icing sugar
- 1 tbsp lemon juice (around ½ small lemon)
- approx. 1 tbsp water
- lemon zest, to decorate (optional)

A home-made custard slice is always a winner at 'take a plate' type events. It looks impressive but isn't expensive to make, particularly when you have access to a lemon tree; alternatively, try your own combo of flavours. I've made it with a classic 'vanilla' custard, it's lovely with passionfruit juice in the custard and glaze, and I've even done a gin and lemon version with a lemon custard and a gin glaze.

1 Preheat the oven to 220°C. Grease a 22–23cm square cake tin, and line it with two long strips of non-stick baking paper placed crosswise to each other so that the paper overhangs on all four sides.

2 Grease two baking trays. Place a sheet of pastry on one tray, prick it all over with a fork, then cover with the other greased tray (greased side down). Place in the oven and weigh down the top tray with a heatproof casserole dish to stop the pastry rising. Bake for 15–20 minutes, till golden. Repeat with the second sheet of pastry.

3 Make the custard. Place the custard powder, sugar, zest and half the milk in a saucepan and whisk until smooth. Add the remaining milk, cream, egg yolk and vanilla and heat gently until simmering, whisking continuously until thick.

4 Remove from the heat, whisk in the lemon juice and set aside for a few minutes to cool slightly but not set. Place the cake tin on top of the pastry sheets and use a sharp knife to trim them so that they will fit neatly inside the tin.

5 Place one pastry sheet in the tin, pour in the custard and level the top. With the best-looking side facing up, place the second pastry sheet on top.

6 Mix the glaze ingredients together with sufficient water to give a spreadable consistency. Pour over the pastry and spread out evenly. Chill for several hours or overnight. Decorate with lemon zest if desired. Slice using a hot, dry serrated knife, wiping the knife between slices.

TIPS: You will need 2–3 large juicy lemons for this recipe.

If you have enough baking trays, bake both pastry sheets at the same time.

NO-BAKE PASSIONFRUIT, LEMON AND GINGERNUT SLICE

READY IN: 40 MINUTES PLUS CHILLING MAKES: AROUND 24 PIECES

- 2 x 250g packets store-bought gingernut biscuits
- 1 cup desiccated coconut
- 150g butter, melted
- 395g can sweetened condensed milk

PASSIONFRUIT CREAM CHEESE TOPPING

- 125g cream cheese
- 3 packed cups icing sugar
- pulp of 3 passionfruit, sieved to remove pips
- 1 tbsp lemon juice
- passionfruit pulp (with pips), to decorate (optional)

Slice tins vary significantly in size; if yours is slightly larger, you will simply get a thinner base and topping, but the overall result will still be fine. However, if you use a smaller tin the quantity might exceed the capacity of your tin. This is a very sweet, tangy treat, so you can get away with serving quite small pieces.

1 Grease and line a 20cm x 30cm Swiss roll or slice tin so that the paper overhangs on all sides.

2 Crush the biscuits to crumbs in a processor or by pounding them in a sturdy bag with a rolling pin. Pour the crushed biscuits, coconut, butter and condensed milk into a bowl, then mix well to combine.

3 Pour the mixture into the prepared tin and press down with your hands. Smooth and neaten by covering with a piece of non-stick baking paper and rolling over the mixture with a can from your pantry. Chill the base in the freezer while you make the topping.

4 For the topping, beat the cream cheese till smooth. Add the icing sugar and mix in. Beat in the sieved passionfruit pulp and lemon juice, and spread over the chilled base. Refrigerate until firm (or slip into the freezer). Drizzle with passionfruit pulp if using.

TIP: You can omit the passionfruit and add extra lemons, or use limes if you have them.

FLUFFY 'WHITE CAKE' WITH WHITE CHOCOLATE FROSTING

READY IN: 1 HOUR PLUS COOLING SERVES: 12

- 1⅓ cups milk
- 20ml white vinegar (1 tbsp + 1 tsp)
- 3⅔ cups plain flour
- ⅓ cup cornflour
- 1¾ tbsp baking powder
- 7 egg whites (see tips)
- 1⅓ cups canola or other neutral-tasting oil
- 2⅓ cups sugar
- 2 tsp vanilla essence (or almond if you prefer)

FROSTING

- ⅓ cup cream, plus 1–2 tbsp extra if needed
- 175g white chocolate, chopped
- 75g butter, at room temperature
- 3½ cups icing sugar

FILLING

- ¼ cup raspberry jam
- 1 tbsp lemon juice
- ¾ cup raspberries, fresh or frozen

'White Cake' is a bit of an American thing, often made from a box mix. I've had many requests over the years to develop a home-made version because they're so pretty – perfect for a baby shower, kitchen tea, etc. So here it is: an easy, pretty and versatile home-made white cake.

I use oil in the batter – it costs less, and omitting both butter and egg yolks results in a pristine white interior. You can use any frosting or filling you like, but the white chocolate and raspberry combo is a good one.

1 Preheat the oven to 180°C. Grease three 20cm loose-bottomed cake tins and dust lightly with flour.

2 Combine the milk and vinegar in a jug and set aside until curdled. Sift the flours and baking powder into a bowl and set aside.

3 Separate the eggs, placing the whites in a large grease-free mixing bowl. Whisk until the mixture will hold a firm peak when the beaters are removed. Set aside.

4 In a large bowl, beat together the oil and sugar for a minute or two, until blended. Add the vanilla, then fold in one-third of the flour followed by one-third of the milk, taking care not to over-mix. Repeat with half the remaining flour and then half the remaining milk, then again with the final amounts of flour and milk.

5 Fold in a quarter of the beaten egg white to loosen the mixture, then fold in the remainder. Divide the batter between the prepared tins, level the tops and bake for 30–35 minutes, until light golden and springy. Cool on a rack before assembling.

6 Make the frosting. Bring the cream to a simmer, add the chopped chocolate and stir till melted. Transfer to a bowl and cool, then beat till light. Beat in the butter, then gradually add the icing sugar and beat in. Add a drop more cream if needed to maintain a spreadable consistency.

RECIPE CONTINUED OVER PAGE

CONTINUED FROM PREVIOUS

7 Make the filling. Heat the jam and lemon juice in a small saucepan. Stir in the raspberries and cool.

8 To assemble, trim the top off each cake to level them. Spread a thin layer of frosting over two of the cakes and pipe a deep dam around the edges of them (see tips), high enough to contain the filling. Fill the centres of the two cake tops with jam filling.

9 Stack the two frosted cakes, then turn the remaining cake upside down and place it on top. Starting in the centre of the top cake, spread frosting all over, working your way down. Smooth the frosting by skimming over with a hot dry spatula.

TIPS: A 'dam' of frosting is a single fat row of frosting that fills the gaps between layers and prevents the filling seeping out. Use a piping bag with a plain nozzle, or cut the corner off a plastic bag; no one will see the dam, so it doesn't need to look pretty.

Leftover egg yolks can be frozen in ones or twos to use later; the chocolate pastry on page 132 uses two, and the custard slice on page 176 and the gingernut cookies on page 166 each use another. If your eggs are bigger than a size 6, use one less.

Mackintosh's
Quality Street
TOFFEES & CHOCOLATES

INDEX

M

N

O

P

Q

R

S

T

V

Z

RANDOM HOUSE

UK | USA | Canada | Ireland | Australia
India | New Zealand | South Africa | China

Random House is an imprint of the Penguin Random House group of companies, whose addresses can be found at global.penguinrandomhouse.com.

Penguin Random House New Zealand

First published by Penguin Random House New Zealand, 2021

3 4 5 6 7 8 9 10

Styling by Sophie Gray and Ingrid Schümann;
props provided by Ingrid Schümann.

Special thanks to Electrolux NZ for providing ovens and kitchen appliances that work as hard as I do, and Award Appliances/Magimix for the only processor that does exactly what it promises.

Design by Cat Taylor © Penguin Random House New Zealand
Cover photograph by Todd Eyre
Prepress by Image Centre Group
Printed and bound in China by Toppan Leefung Printing Limited

A catalogue record for this book is available from the National Library of New Zealand.

ISBN 978-0-14-377544-7

penguin.co.nz

dg
destitutegourmet
— BY SOPHIE GRAY —

FSC
www.fsc.org
MIX
Paper from responsible sources
FSC® C104723